THE SAV
AND
THE SCRIPTURES

A CASE FOR SCRIPTURAL INERRANCY

Robert P. Lightner

BAKER BOOK HOUSE
Grand Rapids, Michigan

Library of Congress
Catalog Card No. 65-27480

ISBN: 0-8010-5581-4

PHOTOLITHOPRINTED BY CUSHING - MALLOY, INC.
ANN ARBOR, MICHIGAN, UNITED STATES OF AMERICA
1978

To the Reverend George P. Atkins
whose dedication to the Lord and the Word
has encouraged me in the ministry.

TABLE OF CONTENTS

FOREWORD

At no time in her history has the Church of God been free from the attacks of the enemy. Satan is many-wiled, and he employs his full arsenal to undermine the people of God and, were it possible, to destroy the Church.

Today he is concentrating upon the very foundation of the Christian Faith, the Word of God. Satan says very many complimentary things about the Word of God, but there is one thing that he demands. We may admire the Scriptures as much as we wish, but we must not insist upon their absolute trustworthiness. And, indeed, the thread of unity that binds together almost all modern discussions of the Bible is that the Bible, whatever else it may be, is not to be regarded as infallible and inerrant.

Professor Lightner's book forms a refreshing contrast to much that is written upon the Bible. We say refreshing advisedly, for the neo-orthodox view of the Bible is really quite dull and uninteresting. It has an air of unreality about it that cannot be completely downed, no matter how orthodox is the phraseology in which it is couched. But the old historic Christian view of inspiration, the view which finds expression in the great creeds of the Church, and, for that matter, in the Bible itself, is full of life and vigor and power.

It is that view which Professor Lightner presents in these pages. Nor does he merely repeat what has been said time and time before. He points out the relevance of the Scriptural view of inspiration for today. His work will create in the heart a deeper love for the Bible and for the Christ of Whom the Bible speaks. If anyone asks, "In the welter of modern opinion, what should I believe about the Bible?" this book will answer his question. May many find their Christian faith strengthened through the reading of this work.

Edward J. Young

Westminster Theological Seminary
Philadelphia, Pennsylvania

INTRODUCTION

This is a book about the most wonderful person and the most wonderful book in the world. Now the world has witnessed a lot of persons and a lot of books and therefore my very first sentence will undoubtedly be challenged. Jesus Christ, the living Word, and the Bible, the written Word, are different from all other persons and books not only in degree but also in kind. Both Christ and the Bible are divinely supernatural. Many are willing to acclaim Christ as a very good man, one who was nearer to God than any other man. He is far more than that; *He is the Son of God.* Likewise many will readily admit that the Bible is a good book, a book containing truth about God. It is far more than that; *it is the Word of God.*

Christ and the Bible are the two impregnable forces upon which Christianity stands or falls. This is true because God, who is ultimate authority, has relegated divine authority to the Bible and Christ is the central theme of Scripture. It is a very popular thing these days to talk about both of these doctrines. Not all of the talk, however, is true to the Bible's testimony about itself and Christ. The truth is that both of these cardinal doctrines of Christianity are under severe attack today.

It is my firm conviction that the present cries of a return to the theology of Jesus and Biblical theology are for the most part not genuine. Very frequently non-conservatives, and all too frequently conservatives, have desired to claim the Saviour while at the same time deviating in varying degrees from His view of Scripture. One hears much these days about the words and deeds of Jesus. Away with Paul, give me Jesus—this is the cry. Jesus and Paul are not in conflict. Paul's view of the inspiration of Scripture expressed in 2 Timothy

3:16 finds perfect agreement with Christ's view expressed in Matthew 5:17, 18 and John 10:33-35. Let us return to the teachings of Jesus but let us not forget what He taught about the Scriptures. You cannot have the Saviour unless you accept His view of the Scriptures also. He will not be divided. His teaching is not open for picking and choosing.

Purpose of the Study

I have two basic purposes for the writing of this book. *First* is the determination of precisely what Christ taught concerning the Scriptures. By no means is Christ's teaching concerning the Scriptures to be viewed as more inspired than other records of Scripture. His words are not to be construed in red-letter fashion as more authoritative than the rest of the Bible. In one sense then, this study is merely one aspect of the Bible's witness to itself. In another sense, however, it is more than that since Christ is the church's Lord and since He said so much about the Scriptures.

This investigation into what Christ explicitly and implicitly taught concerning the Scriptures should provide clear guide lines for the followers of Christ. Certainly, the servant ought not be above his Lord here any more than in any other area. It is hoped that this study will aid in answering the following questions. Has the Christian church been correct in accepting the Scriptures as the infallible revelation of God? Is the orthodox branch of the church right in maintaining that same view today? What view of the Scriptures may the individual justifiably attribute to Christ and thus hold for himself? That Christ's view of Scripture provides a guide for the believer to follow is acknowledged even by those who do not entirely agree with it. T. W. Manson, who is by no means a friend of conservative orthodoxy, was honest enough to admit this fact: "In a word, our Lord's treatment of the Old Testament is based on two things: a profound understanding of the essential teaching of the Hebrew Scriptures and a sure judgement of his own contemporary situation. There is nothing trivial or artificial about his use of the Old Testament: throughout we feel that we are in touch with realities, the realities of divine revelation and the realities of the historical situation. I suggest that this should provide the standard and pattern for our own exegesis of the Old Testament and the New."[1]

Second, this presentation should allow one to evaluate the validity of present day claims of a return to the theology of Jesus and the Bible. Edward J. Young has put the present issue plainly when he said: "Was Jesus, however, justified in so regarding the Old Testament, and are Christians today justified in sharing his opinion? This question is pertinent, indeed; for now, as probably never before, this traditional attitude is being questioned and doubted and attacked. What grounds has the Christian for his belief that the Old Testament Scriptures are the very Word of God? How may he be sure that these writings are indeed authoritative and reliable?"[2]

Pertinence of the Study

Such a study as this, in the science of Biblical theology, is very pertinent to the needs of the present day.

It is pertinent first of all because of the importance of the doctrine of the Scriptures. This is the most important of all doctrines. Objection may be raised by some to such a claim. It is frequently argued that the person and work of Christ are the most important of all Biblical studies. Without any desire to detract from the Saviour it must be said that unless the Biblical record about Him is infallible we have no sure way of knowing whether or not we are believing right things about Him. If God's revelation in the Bible may not be trusted entirely how are we to know when it is to be trusted. If the fountain is corrupt and contaminated so is all the water which flows from it.

Christ is the apex of divine revelation. He is the personification of truth and without Him the Bible would not be complete. If the study of theology could be visualized as a building, the doctrine of the Scriptures would serve as the solid foundation upon which the entire structure rested and

---

[1] T. W. Manson, *The Old Testament in the Teaching of Jesus* (Manchester: The Librarian, The John Rylands Library, 1952), p. 332.

[2] Edward J. Young, "The Authority of the Old Testament," *The Infallible Word,* ed. N. B. Stonehouse and Paul Wooley (Grand Rapids: Wm. B. Eerdmans Publishing Company, 1953), p. 54.

the doctrine of Christ would be seen as the climactic capstone crowning the edifice.

Therefore, regardless of how seriously and piously one may talk about truths contained in the Bible there can be little progress made in these areas unless the Bible is accepted as infallibly authoritative. It is pure theological double-talk and intellectual dishonesty to discredit the authority of the Bible and at the same time to seek refuge in its teachings on other matters, however important they may be.

Secondly, the subject at hand is important because we are witnessing today a resurgence of what is being referred to as "Biblical theology." The rise of neo-orthodoxy has elevated the thinking of contemporary liberalism whereas in classic liberalism there was a candid denial of the worth of the Bible. Liberal theologians of prewar days made no apologies for their denial of the inspiration and authority of the Bible. The pendulum has swung back and now liberals are willing to talk about "rediscovering the Bible," the "theology of Jesus" and "reading the Bible from within." Some of today's liberals wish to condemn the views of their forefathers as heretical. It is because of this new interest in the Bible that many have been deceived into thinking that liberals have turned conservative. There could be no more erroneous conclusion than that. While this study does not deal extensively with the contemporary liberal view of Scripture the study aims to provide the facilities to determine to what extent the "Biblical theology" movement is consistent with the teaching of Christ concerning the Scriptures.

In the third place, the person of Christ makes this study of pertinent value. If He is the apex of God's revelation, if all revelation culminates in Him, then what He said about that revelation is of utmost importance. If He was all that He claimed to be—the divine Son of God—then what He said ought to be obeyed.

The Presuppositions of the Study

The study of any subject proceeds on the assumption of certain presuppositions and this is no less true of the study at hand. There are three basic and underlying presuppositions upon which the writer has based this study.

Concerning the person of Christ

This study proceeds on the premise that Jesus Christ is all that He claimed to be and the New Testament writers made Him out to be—the divine Son of God, very God of very God. The Biblical testimony concerning His perfect humanity is also accepted along with the fact that in the kenosis He did not empty Himself of any attribute of deity which He eternally possessed. Walvoord's summary of this theanthropic person is accepted as true to the Biblical testimony and is the basis upon which this study proceeds. He writes: "In the Person of Christ are two natures, inseparably united, without mixture or loss of separate identity, without loss or transfer of properties or attributes, the union being personal and eternal. The fact that the two natures maintain their complete identity is essential to the doctrine and may be proved without great difficulty. A comparison of the attributes of the human nature and the divine nature will demonstrate that each must belong only to its corresponding nature, though the attributes of either nature belong to the Person of Christ. Because the attributes of either nature belong to Christ, it is proper to refer to His natures as being theanthropic. There is no mixture of the divine and human to form a third substance. The human nature always remains human and the divine nature always remains divine. Christ is therefore both God and man, no less God because of His humanity, and no less human because of His deity."[3]

The acceptance of the above view of Christ means the rejection of the usual explanations of the New Testament teaching concerning Christ's view of Scripture by those who refuse it. Those who deny the view of Scripture which Christ espoused usually base their denial on the following considerations:

The ignorance of Christ: This attempt to invalidate Christ's testimony to the Old Testament ascribes no more knowledge to Christ than that of His contemporaries. Those who hold this view usually argue that His knowledge was adequate for the delivery of doctrines but did not extend to

[3] John F. Walvoord, "Outline of Christology" (unpublished class notes in Christology 106, Dallas Theological Seminary, n.d.), p. 19. (Mimeographed.)

questions of scholarship and criticism. Appeal is usually made to a kenosis theory of incarnation. Packer explains the view: "On this kind of view, the process of incarnation involved such a resignation of divine knowledge on the Son's part that in matters of this kind He inevitably fell victim to the prejudices and errors of His own age. He became a man of His time, it is said, so that naturally His views about the Old Testament were those of His time; but they need not bind us."[4]

This view must be rejected because it does not take into account Christ's claims that what He taught was divine truth. The acceptance of the perfect humanity of Christ precludes the fact that limitations were involved in the incarnation. The Lord did say, "But of that day or that hour knoweth no one, not even the angels in heaven, neither the Son, but the Father" (Mark 13:32). However, in the very immediate context He gave the assurance that what He did say was as unchanging and certain as "heaven and earth" (Mark 13:31). The view under consideration also fails to see the importance and vital place of the Old Testament in Christ's teaching. It assumes that His views of the Old Testament are unessential and can be discarded without loss to His authority.[5]

Tasker has evaluated the fallacy of such an approach to the teachings of Christ: "Indeed, if He could be mistaken on matters which He regarded as of the strictest relevance to His own person and ministry, it is difficult to see exactly how or why He either can or should be trusted anywhere else."[6]

The accommodation of Christ: This attempt to reject Christ's view of the Old Testament will be dealt with more fully in a subsequent chapter. Here the attempt needs only to be defined and stated. Wenham explains this view as follows: "The use of Scripture as a court of appeal in controversy is undoubted, but it again suggests the possibility that Jesus is simply taking His contemporaries on their own ground without committing Himself to the correctness of their prem-

---

[4] J. I. Packer, *"Fundamentalism" and the Word of God* (Grand Rapids: Wm. B. Eerdmans Publishing Co., 1960), p. 60.

[5] *Ibid.*, pp. 60-61.

[6] R. V. G. Tasker, *The Old Testament in the New Testament* (Grand Rapids: Wm. B. Eerdmans Publishing Co., 1963), p. 37.

ises. . . . He deliberately refrained from unsettling them by questioning their conception of the inspiration of their Scriptures, allowing the gentler processes of passing time gradually to bring home to them the imperfect character of what they had hitherto revered."[7]

Even a casual study of the teaching of Christ reveals the fallacy of such a view. Christ did not hesitate to undermine other current beliefs; and furthermore, He maintains the same high view of Scripture even when alone with the disciples, other individuals and even Satan.

As was indicated earlier, these attempts are rejected not only for their own inconsistencies but also because they impair the person of Christ. Any rejection of Christ's view of the Scriptures is an aspersion upon His holy person. Either His testimony is accepted or His deity, integrity and authority must be denied altogether. To reject His authority is to do so on the basis of one's own authority.

Concerning the Scriptures

This discussion will not be occupied with the questions raised by form and source criticism. The conclusions of men like Millar Burrows on this matter are immediately rejected in favor of the Bible's witness to its own inspiration and infallibility. Burrows says: "It is now clear that we cannot reconstruct the order of events in Jesus' life, nor be sure of the settings and contents of his sayings or their exact wording. We cannot even make a list of sayings that are certainly authentic. The church preserved what it found helpful in winning new converts, guiding the life and faith of believers, and meeting the attacks of its enemies."[8]

In contradistinction to this unbelieving subjective viewpoint this study proceeds on the objective testimony of Christ. The author believes firmly in the total inerrancy of Scripture. He believes, without any qualification, that the words of the entire Old and New Testaments in the original autographs are the inspired words of God. This means of course that the

---

[7] J. W. Wenham, *Our Lord's View of the Old Testament* (London: The Tyndale Press, 1953), pp. 18-19.

[8] Millar Burrows, *An Outline of Biblical Theology* (Philadelphia: The Westminster Press, 1946), pp. 46-47.

records which the Gospel writers left us are authentic and authoritative. I believe these men under the guiding control of the Spirit of God wrote what God wanted them to write and what they wrote is the actual record of what happened, not merely what they thought happened or what they interpreted as having happened. When they tell us what Christ said, I believe He said it. They were a lot closer to the events than any critic, be he ancient or modern.

Edward J. Young voiced this present writer's view concerning the nature and end of contemporary subjective criticism when he said: "The subjective nature of these types of criticism will, as time passes, more and more force itself into the open, and the day will come, we believe, when they will be largely discarded as legitimate methods of studying the Bible. At any rate, we shall regard the witness to our Lord which the New Testament offers as completely authoritative."[9]

Concerning the problem of quotations in Christ's teaching

This discussion will not involve a treatment of the sources and variations of quotations in the Lord's teaching of Scripture. It is presupposed, however, that regardless of the source from which He quoted, or the kind of quotation He makes, the words He spoke and which were recorded by the human writers are the very words of God. This is a theological treatment of Christ's teaching of Scripture and not a literary and linguistic one.

It has been argued by some that because of the variations in quotations from the original text of the Old Testament and even from the use of the Septuagint that verbal inspiration is thereby an impossible position. That these variations do not destroy the doctrine of verbal inspiration is proven by the consideration of several facts. First of all it cannot always be determined when a direct quotation is intended. Johnson argues that quotations were sometimes given from memory, some were fragmentary, some were quotations of substance and some by sound.[10]

---

[9] Young, *op. cit.*, p. 55.

[10] Franklin Johnson, *The Quotations of the New Testament from the Old Considered in the Light of General Literature* (Philadelphia: American Baptist Publication Society, 1896), pp. 1-185.

Secondly, all the words of the end product are inspired whether it is a complete and perfect quotation or not. Thirdly, the Spirit of God must be allowed total freedom to modify and select expressions which He inspired in the Old Testament.

Ladd has summarized Christ's method of quoting and the variations which exist: "But there is no proof that in quoting Hebrew prophecy Jesus thought it necessary to confine himself to the exact words, or exclusively to either the Hebrew text or that of the LXX.: sometimes he departs from all known texts, with no assignable reason for his departure."[11]

It is an interesting and illuminating fact that Christ did not have the originals but only versions and copies and thus His quotations of necessity came from these. It is also significant that no one ever questioned His references or accused Him of misquoting Scripture.

Often Christ's quotations, whether from the Hebrew or the Greek, were free (John 8:17; Matt. 19:5; 22:37-39). Sometimes they were of an interpretive nature (Matt. 11:10; Luke 7:27). On still other occasions He chose from the prophecy that which emphasized His meaning (Matt. 26:31; 15:7-9). Sometimes He combined the Hebrew and the Septuagint version (Matt. 15:9; cf. Isa. 29:13). In Matthew 13:14-16 He gave preference to the Greek version in order to emphaize His point.[12]

Roger Nicole has dealt extensively with this matter of quotations not only in Christ's teaching but also in the entire New Testament. His principles in explanation of the variations and in defense of verbal inspiration in light of the variations will be cited here: "1. The New Testament writers had to translate their quotations. 2. The New Testament writers did not have the same rules for quotations as are nowadays enforced in works of a scientific character. 3. The New Testament writers sometimes paraphrased their quotations. 4. The New Testament writers often simply alluded to Old Testament passages without intending to quote them. 5. The New Testa-

---

[11] George T. Ladd, *The Doctrine of Sacred Scripture* (New York: Charles Scribner's Sons, 1883), I, 71.

[12] Pierre Ch. Marcel, "Our Lord's Use of Scripture," *Revelation and the Bible*, ed. Carl F. H. Henry (Grand Rapids: Baker Book House, 1958), p. 122.

ment authors sometimes recorded quotations made by others. 6. Other principles whose application must be limited."[13]

Obviously each of the above principles does not apply in every case of the Lord's quotations. However, they do provide, either as a group or individually, a satisfactory explanation for the variations and apparent discrepancies in Christ's use of the Old Testament.

Acknowledgments

The present work is a revision of a doctor's dissertation presented to the faculty of Dallas Theological Seminary and Graduate School of Theology under the title "The Bibliology of Christ." The author wishes to express appreciation to the faculty for their kind permission to publish this material.

A word of acknowledgment is due also to Mr. Charles H. Craig and Professor Robert L. Reymond of the Presbyterian and Reformed Publishing Company for valuable suggestions regarding content and style.

Of necessity many passages will be referred to often but each chapter will deal with the central passages involved and will seek to establish the Saviour's teaching on the particular point at hand.[14]

---

[13] Roger Nicole, "New Testament Use of the Old," *Revelation and the Bible*, ed. Carl F. H. Henry (Grand Rapids: Baker Book House, 1958), pp. 142-47.

[14] Unless otherwise indicated all Scripture quotations are taken from *The Holy Bible*, ed. American Revision Committee (New York: Thomas Nelson & Sons, 1901). Permission for quotations is gratefully recognized.

CHAPTER I

THE USE OF SCRIPTURE IN THE SAVIOUR'S TEACHING

Christ viewed the Old Testament Scriptures as a harmonious unit and an organic whole. The conviction held by the Christian church that the Old Testament is an infallible revelation of God was shared by the Lord Himself. He appealed to the Scriptures constantly. Christ's frequent and extensive use extends not only to the Scripture as a whole but also to individual parts, words and letters. Edward J. Young has stated this succinctly: "Not only did Jesus Christ look upon the Old Testament as forming an organic whole but also he believed that both as a unit and in its several parts it was finally and absolutely authoritative. . . . Not only, however, was such authority attributed to the Scriptures as a unit and to particular verses or utterances, but it was also extended to include individual words and even letters."[1]

It is indeed significant that Christ never even so much as referred to the extra-Biblical literature of His day. Many works existed to which He had access and He could have made reference to them but did not do so. He relied solely upon the Old Testament canon of Scripture. Christ always assumed the unquestionable truthfulness and complete trustworthiness of the Holy Scriptures. With divine fervency and frequency He declared its final authority and absolute inviolability. The Saviour's attitude toward Scripture, His purposes in using Scripture, His extensive use of Scripture and His methods of interpretation and application, all portray His reverent regard for the Word of God.

---

[1] Edward J. Young, "The Authority of the Old Testament," *The Infallible Word*, ed. N. B. Stonehouse and Paul Wooley (Grand Rapids: Wm. B. Eerdmans Publishing Company, 1953), pp. 56-57.

His Exclusive Use of the Hebrew Canon

Tradition rejected

Christ candidly rejected the Jewish traditions which contradicted Scripture. A casual reading of the Gospel records will reveal His frequent reference to the traditions of men. Whenever He spoke of them He always coupled with His reference His own estimate of their inferiority to the Scriptures. He frequently spoke of the "traditions of the elders," which were popularly associated with the Scriptures. However, whenever He spoke of them He did so to discredit their equally binding force. He said: "Ye reject the commandment of God, that ye may keep your tradition" (Mark 7:9).

The traditions of the elders which were rejected by Christ were those which marred the Word of God. "In many points He condemned the Jewish tradition, but not with respect to the canonicity of Scripture. His complaint, indeed, was that by other traditions they had invalidated in practice the Word of God recorded in canonical Scripture."[2]

Apocrypha neglected

A further proof of His exclusive use of the Hebrew canon is His complete neglect of the Apocryphal writings which were in existence and available for His use. These were the books which were not included in the list of inspired books and were not accorded an equal place of authority along with the books of the Old Testament.

That these literatures existed in His day is an agreed fact by scholars. The extreme limits between which all of these non-inspired books were completed is some time between 300 B.C. and A.D. 100. In response to the query of why these books were not accorded the same authority as canonical books by Christ or His apostles, Bruce makes this observation: "The answer is rather that they were not regarded as canonical by the Jews, either of Palestine or of Alexandria; and that our Lord and His apostles accepted the Jewish canon and confirmed its authority by the use they made of it, whereas there is no evidence to show that they regarded the apocry-

[2] F. F. Bruce, *The Books and the Parchments* (London: Pickering and Inglis Ltd., 1950), p. 102.

phal literature (or as much of it as had appeared in their time) as similarly authoritative."[3]

Septuagint used

Christ frequently quoted from the Septuagint. The Septuagint with dates ranging from about 250 to 160 B.C. is a Greek translation of the Old Testament. Christ used the Septuagint frequently in His quotations and references to the Old Testament.

The use of the Septuagint was widespread in Christ's day. Its popularity in the ancient world would probably compare with the popularity of the Authorized Version in our day. Christ's use of the Septuagint in no way indicates that He thought that version to be inspired. He did not confer inspiration upon it and the contention that Christ's usage of the Septuagint militates against the theory of verbal inspiration is unfounded. The fact of the matter is that verbal inspiration relates only to the original autographs and those were not in existence at the time of Christ and thus whenever He does quote from the Hebrew it is from a copy of the original autograph. Neither is it to be implied that Christ was obligated to always quote from the Septuagint.

The writers of the New Testament used the Septuagint in many of their quotations from the Old Testament. "Whenever they wanted to emphasize an idea which was insufficient or inadequately rendered in the LXX, they may have retranslated in whole or in part the passage in question. In certain cases the reason for their introduction of changes may remain unknown to us, but we are not on that account in a position to say either that a careful reproduction of the LXX is illegitimate or that a modification of that text is unjustifiable."[4]

There are three basic views regarding the use of the Septuagint by New Testament writers. Some hold that they always made use of the Septuagint, others that they quoted solely from the Hebrew text, and still others that they ad-

---

[3] *Ibid.*, p. 164.

[4] Roger Nicole, "The New Testament Use of the Old," *Revelation and the Bible*, ed. Carl F. H. Henry (Grand Rapids: Baker Book House, 1958), p. 144.

hered uniformly to neither but used the one and the other in accordance with their purpose. Each case must be determined on the basis of the facts involved.

Testimony of the Gospel records

The Gospel records bear testimony to the fact that Christ quoted solely from the Scriptures, sometimes from the existing Hebrew copies and sometimes from the Septuagint or Greek translation. His canon (list of books) of Scripture was identical with the Hebrew canon and He declared Himself in complete agreement with its bounds by referring to it as Law, Prophets and Psalms (Luke 24:44). This tripartite division of the Old Testament He referred to as "the Scriptures" (Luke 24:45).

His General Attitude in the Use of Scripture

The knowledge of the Scriptures which Christ possessed is demonstrated by His use of them. His attitude was one of reverence for the Old Testament Scripture and He had a profound respect for its inherent authority. He held the law to be inviolable and the entire Scripture as that which could not be annulled. Christ's frequent and continued appeal to the Scriptures reveals His attitude toward them.

Many of the Scriptures used in this section will necessarily be dealt with in more detail in subsequent chapters. The purpose here is to show in broad perspective Christ's attitude as He used the Scripture.

Scripture of divine origin

This attitude of Christ toward Scripture is foundational to His entire view. All the other concepts and attitudes which He taught are dependent upon this one and rest upon it for their validity.

The Scriptures are the "commandment of God" (Mark 7:8, 9, 13). The phrase "commandment of God" is significant here since He is contrasting it with the "tradition of men." He is thus making a distinction between God's Word and man's word. Christ calls the "commandment of God" the "word of God" (Mark 7:13).

According to Christ's words in Mark 12:36 the Scriptures are the product of the Holy Spirit: "David himself said in the Holy Spirit." When speaking of the law Christ said "God commanded" (Matt. 15:3).

Thus it is seen that Christ maintained the Scriptures to be of divine origin. More will be said on this aspect of His teaching when His teaching of the revelation of Scripture is examined.

Scripture enduring

There are at least three central passages in which Christ speaks of the eternal character of the Scriptures. In each case the durability and eternality of Scripture is compared with heaven and earth (Matt. 5:17, 18; 24:35; Luke 16:16, 17). In the clearest and strongest language possible Christ said, "But it is easier for heaven and earth to pass away, than for one tittle of the law to fail" (Luke 16:17). This comparison of Scripture with the continuance of the physical creation elevates the Scriptures to such an extent that they cannot be accounted for apart from a supernatural origin.

Scripture inviolable

The classic passage in which Christ expresses this attitude toward the Old Testament Scriptures is John 10:35, "The Scripture cannot be broken." The context reveals Christ advancing divine claims and as a result the Jews, with a full understanding of the claims, charge Him with blasphemy. In justification of His claim to be the Son of God He quotes Psalm 82:6. This is not merely an expression of the attitude of the Jews to Scripture; it is the Saviour's own claim for the inviolability of Scripture. Without any question Christ here views the law as Scripture and as that which is irrefragable, indefectible and inviolable.

Scripture prophetic in character

The phrase "that it might be fulfilled" or its equivalent is a frequent expression of Christ concerning the Scripture. In His usage He not only taught His own part in the fulfillment of Scripture but He also taught how Scripture was fulfilled by and for the benefit of others. What oftentimes appeared to be an occasional happening He said came to pass "that the Scripture might be fulfilled" (Mark 14:49; John 13:18; 17:12). The truth which the Lord wanted to convey by His oft-repeated "that it might be fulfilled" was the certainty of the Scriptures. No detail, however insignificant or even unnecessary of a literal fulfillment it may have appeared to others, ever escaped His notice or sanction.

Scripture worthy of acceptance

Both by example and exhortation Christ taught that the Scripture was to be accepted. The divine origin and the enduring, inviolable and prophetic character of Scripture establish the worthiness of its acceptance. Scripture was to be accepted because it came from God in contradistinction to the "tradition" which came from men. The very fact that He accepted for Himself without any reservations the entire Old Testament canon (Matt. 23:35; Luke 24:44) implies the fact that He intended others to so accept it.

The point which Christ is seeking to make with the Jews in John 5 is that they had not believed or accepted Moses else they would have believed Him (John 5:46). The problem with the scribes and Pharisees was their selectivity with regard to the Scripture and particularly the Mosaic law portion of it. They only accepted that which suited them and the rest they neglected. For this procedure Christ chides them sternly: "Woe unto you, scribes and Pharisees, hypocrites! for ye tithe mint and anise and cummin, and have left undone the weightier matters of the law, justice, and mercy, and faith: but these ye ought to have done, and not to have left the other undone" (Matt. 23:23).

Christ's observation is to the effect that the overly conscientious scrupulosity of the Pharisees, with regard to tithing, had driven them to a complete neglect of the weightier matters of the law. They had done the lesser and neglected the greater. His point is, both things ought to have been done because both are in the law. Thus, here and on many other occasions Christ taught that the Scripture was to be accepted and obeyed.

Christ's general attitude then concerning Scripture reveals His explicit faith in it as the divine revelation of God. As such it was eternal, inviolable, prophetic in character and thus worthy of acceptance.

THE FORMULAS AND TITLES EMPLOYED IN THE USE OF SCRIPTURE

Most of the formulas and titles which Christ used to introduce and refer to Scripture are familiar. However, the meaning of each of them is often overlooked. Also, the significance of them is of great importance because of the emphasis which Christ placed upon them in His use of Scripture.

The various formulas and titles will be presented, followed by a brief discussion of the significance of their usage by Christ.

The general formulas and titles

Scripture and Scriptures: All the Gospel writers record instances of the Saviour referring to the Scriptures, sometimes in the singular, "scripture," and sometimes in the plural, "scriptures." This is the most common name for the Old Testament. Christ always employed this title in a strictly restricted sense by always referring to the sacred writings as distinguished from the profane writings.[5] The reference in John 10:35 is singular and refers to the whole of Scripture. On other occasions He uses the singular "scripture" and points to one particular passage (Luke 4:21). Again, in John 5:39 His reference to the "scriptures" is clearly a reference to the entirety of the Old Testament.

Law and commandments: The terms law and commandments in their various forms are sometimes used interchangeably by the Lord. In most instances He restricts the term "law" to the Mosaic legislation and frequently identifies it with Moses the law-giver (Luke 22:44; John 7:19, 23). Christ's reference is not always restricted to the Mosaic law however. He sometimes applies "law" to other portions of

[5] The word is always so used in the New Testament with the single exception of Peter's reference to Paul's epistles as Scripture (2 Pet. 3:16).

the Old Testament as in John 10:34 where He quotes Psalm 82:6 and identifies it as "law."

Christ defines His attitude to the commandments in the Sermon on the Mount (Matt. 5:17-48), in His criticism of Pharisaic tradition (Matt. 15:1, 20; Mark 7:1-23), in His reply to the rich young ruler (Matt. 19:17-21; Mark 10:19-21; Luke 18:20-22), in His dialogue with the lawyer (Matt. 22:35-40; Mark 12:28, 34; Luke 10:25-37), and in His treatment of the Sabbath commandment (Mark 2:24-27, Luke 6:1-10; 13:10-16). In each of these instances He has nothing but the highest regard for the commandments of God.

Law, Prophets and Psalms: The Lord's use of "law" has been discussed above but it remains to be seen that Christ also used the formulas, "prophets" and "psalms" in His use of Scripture. This threefold designation refers of course to the three main divisions of the Old Testament. Whatever may be said of one may be said of all. These titles are used interchangeably and they denote the collection of sacred writings in the Old Testament.

It is written: The word γέγραπται is often used in the New Testament to describe Christ's means of referring to the prophetic Scriptures of the Old Testament. The most familiar occurrences are in the temptation accounts (Matt. 4:1-11; Mark 1:12, 13; Luke 4:11-13). It is indeed significant that the verb in this formula always appears in some form of the perfect tense, passive voice, indicative mood or participle. Vincent translates it in Matthew 4:4: "It *has been* written, and *stands* written."[6] Thus, Matthew here presents Christ as one who believed in the finality and irrevocable nature of the Old Testament revelation. Because of the relevance of the temptation experience to Christ's teaching concerning Scripture, reference will be made to it again.

Have ye not read? This formula comes from the word ἀνέγνωτε. When it occurs with the negative it is translated "Have ye not read?" The word occurs frequently in Christ's dealing with His critics. Whenever He uses the phrase He speaks of an Old Testament passage with which they should have been familiar, and probably were, but had

[6] Marvin R. Vincent, *Word Studies in the New Testament* (New York: Charles Scribner's Sons, 1924), I, 28.

missed the true meaning. According to Greek grammar, when the negative οὐκ, οὐδέποτε, or οὐδέ is "used in a question its use always implies that the expected answer is 'yes.'"[7] Thus, Christ is implying by his question of introduction that His critics had read but had not understood the Scripture referred to.

That it might be fulfilled: This phrase is not always used as a formula. However, in many instances Christ does so use it either in relation to Himself or in relation to others. The phrase when used as a formula does not always precede the Scripture referred to. Sometimes the Scripture is cited or referred to and the phrase "that it might be fulfilled" or an equivalent phrase follows (Matt. 26:56; John 17:12).

A study of the contexts in which this formula occurs reveals that Christ did not always intend by its use to make a direct quotation. Sometimes the quotations are paraphrased, sometimes the passage is only alluded to and on other occasions there is a direct quotation. Whatever the case may be, the Spirit of God must be allowed freedom to modify or alter the expressions He inspired in the Old Testament.

The Word of God: Scripture is expressly called "the word of God" by Christ in John 10:35: "If ye called them gods, unto whom the word of God came (and the scripture cannot be broken)." The reference which Christ makes to the Psalms as Jewish law is clearly an identification of it with the Word of God. Christ here calls a passage in Psalms "law," "word of God" and "scripture." They were all one and the same in His mind and He used the terms interchangeably.

The Saviour did not always use an introductory formula in His reference to Scripture. Many times He undoubtedly quoted or referred to the Old Testament without any special designation.

The significance of the use of the formulas and titles

These formulas and titles are significant for the following reasons. *First,* they reveal Christ's attitude toward the Old

---

[7] E. H. Dana and Julius R. Mantey, *A Manual Grammar of the Greek New Testament* (New York: The Macmillan Company, 1947), p. 264.

Testament. For Him these technical designations spoke of the authoritative revelation of God deposited in the Old Testament. These introductory phrases and words were used exclusively of the Word.

Thus, tribute is paid to the divine authority and origin of Scripture. The Word was the communication of God to man. An illustration of this significance is seen in the formula "It is written." Concerning this formula Warfield observes: "The simple adduction in this solemn and decisive manner of a written authority, carries with it the implication that the appeal is made to the indefectible authority of the Scriptures of God, which in all their parts and in every one of their declarations are clothed with the authority of God Himself."[8]

Second, Christ's usage of these formulas shows His knowledge and familiarity not only of portions of the Scripture but also of the whole Old Testament. Not only is His knowledge and familiarity revealed by these terms but also His acceptance of the entire Old Testament Scripture. Without any attempt to alter or debate its contents He accepted the Scriptures.

Third, His usage of these formulas and titles supposes the existence of a complete collection of writings distinct from all others. The Saviour always used these to refer to the canonical Scriptures. They do not set the boundaries of the canon; yet they do suppose the existence of a body of writings which was separate and fixed in distinction from other literature.

His Purposes in the Use of Scripture

The purposes for which Christ used the Scriptures are many and varied. There are of course general purposes such as His desire and determination to please the Father and do His will. Also, His interest in the welfare of mankind would serve as an adequate purpose for His frequent and exalted use of Scripture.

There are specific purposes, however, in Christ's usage and these will now be examined. It will be seen that some of

---

[8] Benjamin Breckinridge Warfield, *The Inspiration and Authority of the Bible* (Philadelphia: The Presbyterian and Reformed Publishing Company, 1958), p. 240.

these purposes relate to Christ Himself, some to His friends and some to His enemies.

In relation to Himself

It is certain that Jesus did not come to supersede or replace the Scriptures. His purpose was not to substitute His own authority for the authority of Scripture.

Christ not only endorsed Biblical authority by His application of it to others but He too submitted to its authority. He avowed to obey what was written (Matt. 4:1ff.; Luke 4:1ff.; Matt. 16:21-23). He claimed for Himself and His disciples the obedience of the law. The problem was not that Jesus and His disciples had disobeyed the law but that their critics, the Pharisees, had grossly misunderstood the law's true meaning (Mark 2:24ff.; 3:4f.; Luke 13:14ff.; John 7:21ff.)

Christ had several outstanding purposes in His use of Scripture for Himself:

To express His own faith: Every reference, direct or indirect, which Christ makes to the Scriptures may be taken as an expression of His complete faith and trust in them. There are instances though where He quotes Scripture to express His own faith and feelings. The Psalmist makes general use of the expression "Into thine hand I commit my spirit" (Ps. 31:5) and this expression is referred to by Christ on the cross in His dying moments (Luke 23:46). His usage at that time reveals something of His estimation of the Scripture and His own confidence in it even while He is giving His life for sinners. Again, the Lord quotes Psalm 22:1 during the three hours of darkness while He was on the cross (Matt. 27:46). As in the other instance so here Christ is demonstrating His reliance upon the words of the Old Testament, His faith in the Scriptures, even in the hour of death.

The entire life and ministry of Christ was an expression of His faith in and dependence upon the Scriptures. M'Intosh states: ". . . He tells us that His own preaching in Nazareth, going up to Jerusalem to die, teaching by parables, working of miracles, the betrayal by Judas, denial of Peter, forsaking of Him by all, the seizure of Him by the Jews, condemnation by Jews and Gentiles, put to death and rising from the dead—

with many of the details of His whole life, work and sufferings—were foretold and predetermined by Scripture . . . ."[9]

Thus it is seen that Christ took the Scriptures as His own life guide. He also found in the Scriptures His spiritual nourishment and sustenance. His lifework was performed under its inspiration, temptations resisted by its strength, life crises endured by its sustaining power. He lived, labored, suffered and died with a total commitment to its authority. The Saviour in His person and work was so committed to and identified with Scripture that He and the Scripture stand or fall together.

To defend His views: This fact is all the more significant in view of His claims to speak with divine authority and His right to set aside the traditions of the fathers, which claims and right He received from His Father. Especially is this true in view of the extravagant regard which His contemporaries held for the traditions of men.

In defense of His views respecting marriage and divorce He quotes Genesis 2:23, 24 (Matt. 19:5). He quotes Isaiah 6:9, 10 to justify His parabolic ministry (Matt. 13:13, 15; Luke 8:10; cf. John 12:39, 40).

Matthew 22:32 is a quotation from Exodus 3:6, 15 and sustains His teaching about the resurrection. The Lord does not make use of the historical application of the setting in Exodus but uses the words of Moses to show that Abraham, Isaac and Jacob were alive at the time He spoke the words and would ever be alive. Christ's argument here is that since the Lord was the God of the patriarchs they thus are assured of immortality and immortality certainly demands the resurrection of the body.

When Jesus found it necessary to defend His doctrine respecting the need of a divine and effectual call in order that men may come to Him, He refers to Isaiah 54:13 (John 6:45). Isaiah had predicted that the true Israelites would be disciples of Jehovah, not of human leaders. Christ takes this prediction and applies it to Himself as the one who gives life.

To sustain His claims: Only brief reference needs to be made here to the times when Christ defended His claims by reference to the Scripture.

---

[9] Hugh M'Intosh, *Is Christ Infallible and the Bible True?* (Edinburgh: T. & T. Clark, 1901), p. 207.

Christ's favorite title for Himself, Son of Man, is taken from Psalm 8:4; Daniel 7:13 and Ezekiel 1:26. His claims to be the Good Shepherd in John 10:2-5, 10-16 summarizes such passages as Genesis 49:24; Psalm 23:1; 8:1; Isaiah 40:11; Jeremiah 3:15; 23:4; Ezekiel 34:23; 37:24 and Zechariah 13:7.

The Saviour cites Psalm 110:1 in Matthew 22:41-45 and thus shows the superiority of the Messiah to David since He was David's Lord and David's Son. By His argument from the less to the greater Christ sustains His claim to the title Son of God (John 10:34-36). This claim He bases upon Psalm 82:6 and the historical reference in Exodus 22:28.

The nature of His ministry He defends by precise quotation from Isaiah's prophecy (Luke 4:17-19; cf. Isa. 61:1ff.). To illustrate and prefigure His future death and resurrection Christ relates the account of Jonah and his experience (Matt. 12:40; cf. Jonah). Tasker ably summarizes this aspect of Christ's use of the Old Testament: "In our Lord's judgment the Old Testament foreshadowed the part which He Himself was to play in bringing to its glorious climax the divine plan for man's salvation. 'Moses, the Prophets, and the Psalms,' as He subdivided the contents of the Old Testament (Lk. 24:44), all contained 'things concerning Himself'; and in consequence they were the vital and determining factor in the shaping and the fulfillment of His divine vocation."[10]

In relation to others

Christ frequently found occasion to express wonder at the limited knowledge which His contemporaries had of the Scriptures and the effect which the Scriptures had upon their lives. In sorrow the Lord said "Ye search the scriptures, because ye think that in them ye have eternal life; and these are they which bear witness of me" (John 5:39). Warfield's comment on this passage is to the point: " 'Ye search the scriptures'—that is right: and 'even you' (emphatic) 'think to have eternal life in them'—that is right, too. But 'it is these very Scriptures' (very emphatic) 'which are bearing witness' (continuous process) 'of me; and' (here is the mar-

[10] R. V. G. Tasker, *Our Lord's Use of the Old Testament* (London: Pickering and Inglis Ltd., 1953), p. 3.

vel) 'ye will not come to me and have life!'—that you may, that is, reach the very end you have so properly in view in searching the Scriptures. Their failure is due, not to the Scriptures but to themselves, who read the Scriptures to such little purpose."[11]

Christ's attitude toward those among whom He ministered regarding their knowledge of the Scriptures is revealed in such phrases as, "Have ye not read even this scripture" (Mark 12:10), "Yea, did you never read" (Matt. 21:16), "Ye do err, not knowing the scriptures, nor the power of God" (Matt. 22:29). Others could be added to this testimony but these are sufficient to teach that Christ believed the religious leaders of His day to be ignorant of the Old Testament Scriptures and their true meaning.

Thus, Christ used the Scripture itself to show them their lack of perception of it and their need for a thorough understanding of its revelation of Him. Christ had specific purposes in mind as He used the Scriptures with His disciples and with His enemies.

Use with His disciples: The frequent use of Scripture by Christ to combat the errors of His enemies is expected since He was attempting to vindicate His claims and bring conviction to their hearts. The purposes for His use of Scripture with His own was altogether different. He had a special and intimate relation to His carefully chosen disciples and to these He gave personal and instructive teaching in the Scriptures.

When he spoke to the multitudes in parables His disciples asked Him privately the reason for such ministry. He replied by quoting the prophecy of Isaiah 6:9, 10 and declared His conviction that the prophets were righteous men (Matt. 13:10-14).

During the latter part of His life on earth Christ spoke to His disciples often concerning His part in the fulfillment of the prophetic Word. Luke 18:31-33 is illustrative of Christ's attitude toward His death and His desire to instruct the disciples in Scripture. "And he took unto him the twelve, and said unto them, Behold, we go up to Jerusalem, and all the things that are written through the prophets shall be accomplished unto the Son of man. For he shall be delivered up unto

---

[11] Warfield, *op. cit.*, p. 142.

the Gentiles, and shall be mocked, and shamefully treated, and spit upon: and they shall scourge and kill him: and the third day he shall rise again."

Likewise, after His resurrection when He appeared to His own He directs their attention again to the Old Testament prophecies concerning Himself. The two on the road to Emmaus had their doubts dissipated and their gloom dispelled when Jesus interpreted to them from Moses and all the prophets things concerning Himself (Luke 24:27). Not only was this message given to the two on the road to Emmaus but the same message was also given to the other disciples gathered in Jerusalem. The Lord reminded the entire group that ". . . all things must needs be fulfilled, which are written in the law of Moses, and the prophets, and the psalms, concerning me (Luke 24:44). These were His most intimate friends, those whom He loved and those to whom He desired to reveal His inner most thoughts. It is to these that we find Him revealing His sublime faith in the authority, power and blessedness of Scripture. His view of Scripture remains unaltered whether He is rebuking Satan alone in the wilderness or whether He is comforting His sorrowing disciples.

Use with His enemies: The authority which Christ assigned to the Old Testament inevitably brought Him into direct opposition and conflict with the majority of the Jews of His day. In fact, the supreme authority which He assigned to the Word of God is best observed in His disputes with His religious enemies.

There are three basic purposes which Christ had in His use of Scripture with His enemies:

First, it is obvious that Christ was on many occasions defending His actions. The classic illustration of this purpose is found in Matthew 12:1-8 where the Lord answers the criticism of the Pharisees regarding the plucking of grain on the Sabbath. The argument of the Pharisees was not over the act of plucking the ears of corn and eating them but the fact that this plucking and eating was done on the Sabbath.

There are other occasions where criticism was leveled against Christ by His foes and He defended Himself by recourse to the Scripture. Matthew 12:10 and Luke 14:3 relate to the Sabbath issue and demonstrate Christ's rejection of the "traditions of the elders."

Likewise, the experiences of the cleansing of the temple and the acclamation of praise which followed (Matt. 21:12-13) are illustrative of Christ's scriptural defense before His enemies.

Second, Christ's purpose in the use of Scripture with His enemies was to denounce their error. To all who in wilful ignorance made false assumptions and wrong deductions from Scripture and relied on the tradition of men Christ said: "This people honoreth me with their lips, But their heart is far from me. But in vain do they worship me, teaching as their doctrines the precepts of men" (Mark 7:6-7; Isa. 29:13). The Pharisees and scribes, to whom the above rebuke was given, transgressed the commandment of God because of their tradition (Matt. 15:3). This error of traditionalism was the chief error which the Lord had to combat, and the above passage clearly reveals Christ's attitude toward it.

With regard to the Sadducees' denial of the resurrection Christ declared "Ye do err" (Matt. 22:29). They erred in not knowing that God is the God of the living. They searched the Scriptures but had missed the real meaning (John 5:39). Because of the strong adherence on the part of the Pharisees to the traditions of their fathers they naturally rejected the Christ of whom the Scriptures spoke and that was their most damning error (Matt. 21:23-46).

The error of hypocrisy might also be listed. Their error of hypocrisy stemmed from an omission of "weightier matters of the law" (Matt. 23:23).

Third, Christ used the Scriptures to declare His own relation to them before His enemies. The error of unbelief was made obvious by Christ as He stripped the Jews of any possible hold on the Father, the Scriptures, or Moses since they had rejected Him of whom Moses wrote. The Saviour said to the Jews, "Search the scriptures for in them ye think ye have eternal life: and they are they which testify of me" (John 5:39). This is not a condemnation for searching the Scriptures to find eternal life. It is rather an accusation upon them for not seeing Christ in the Old Testament. Eternal life is not found in the words of Scripture but in the one of whom those words speak.

Since a more extended section will be devoted to the fulfillment of Scripture in Christ it will not be necessary to labor the point here. Suffice it to say that in His judgment the Old

Testament foreshadowed the part He was to play in the divine plan for man's salvation. Moses, the Prophets and the Psalms contained "things concerning Himself" (Luke 24:44).

THE EXTENT OF HIS USE OF SCRIPTURE

His knowledge of Scripture

Since Christ was the divine Son of God He had a complete and total knowledge of all things. The testimony of John is that He knew "what was in man" (John 2:25).

The condescension of Christ brought Him into the sphere of certain human limitations. He was truly God and perfect man. But He was a man. It is with this fact of His humanity in mind that Luke writes: "And Jesus advanced in wisdom and stature, and in favor with God and men" (Luke 2:52).

Christ was a student of the Scriptures, of men and of things as long as He was on earth and thus subject to the limitations of human life. No doubt His mother Mary taught Him orally at home. Mary was well acquainted with the Old Testament according to her magnificat (Luke 1:46-55). The impartation of Scriptural knowledge by the parents to the children was considered vital and a natural part of Jewish life. "But while the earliest religious teaching would, of necessity, come from the lips of the mother, it was the father who was 'bound to teach his son.' To impart to the child knowledge of the Torah conferred as great spiritual distinction, as if a man had received the Law itself on Mount Horeb."[12]

Added to this home training in the Scripture would be the synagogue worship. Here prayers were offered, the Shema recited and benedictions pronounced which were all based on Scriptural phrases. The synagogue services were celebrated three or four times a week thus making more accessible the knowledge of the Old Testament. It is said that the Jews would more readily tell about their laws than tell their own names.

That Christ read from the Old Testament is certain from Luke 4:16, Matthew 5:18, and Luke 16:17. Luke declares that He read from the prophet Isaiah (Luke 4:17). Accord-

---

[12] Alfred Edersheim, *The Life and Times of Jesus the Messiah* (London: Longmans, Green, and Co., 1912), I, 230.

ing to Matthew 5:18 and Luke 16:17 He was familiar with the alphabetical structure of the language.

The knowledge of Scripture which He possessed was revealed early in His life. The incident in the temple related in Luke 2:41-52 indicates that at the age of twelve He had a baffling knowledge of Scripture. He knew how to ask and how to answer the questions (Matt. 12:3).

The wide use which Christ makes of the Scripture certainly reveals His knowledge of it. His entire life and ministry was saturated with reference to the Scripture. Some believe that it is not at all unlikely that Jesus knew the Old Testament by heart from Genesis to Malachi. Perhaps this is an overstatement. However, He was thoroughly acquainted with the entire Old Testament both in Hebrew and Greek and doubtless committed much of it to memory.

His extensive use of Scripture

The passages and portions of Scripture to which Jesus referred are many and varied. Never once did He ever question the integrity of the human authors or the authority of what they wrote.

According to the count of Graham Scroggie there are 1934 verses out of the 3779 in the Authorized Version of the Gospels which contain in whole or in part words of Christ.[13] Many of these verses are occupied with reference to or about the Old Testament. Rimmer observes that ". . . 179 verses are literal Old Testament words. Ten percent of the daily conversation of Jesus was Old Testament verses literally quoted."[14]

A brief survey of the Old Testament books which Christ directly referred to will be helpful in showing the variety of Scripture used by Him and the circumstances under which He used them.

Genesis is referred to in connection with the marriage relationships (Matt. 19:4, 5; Mark 10:6-8). According to the Genesis account Moses was speaking; yet Christ said the Creator spoke the words.

---

[13] W. Graham Scroggie, *A Guide to the Gospels* (London: Pickering & Inglis Ltd., 1948), p. 193.

[14] Harry Rimmer, *Internal Evidence of Inspiration* (Grand Rapids: Wm. B. Eerdmans Publishing Co., 1938), p. 227.

Exodus is quoted by Christ in connection with Moses and the burning bush (Matt. 22:32; Mark 12:26) and many other incidents (Matt. 5:21, 27; 15:4; Mark 7:10; Matt. 19:18, 19; Mark 10:19).

Portions of Leviticus are used by Christ to teach the proper relation of ceremonial regulations (Matt. 5:33, 43; 19:19; 22:39; Mark 12:31; Luke 10:27).

The story of the brazen serpent referred to by Christ in His conversation with Nicodemus is found in the book of Numbers (Num. 21:9; cf. John 3:14).

Quotations of Christ from the book of Deuteronomy are found in many places (Mark 12:29, 30; Matt. 22:37; Luke 10:27).

Five of the Prophets are directly quoted by Christ. These Prophets are Isaiah, Jeremiah, Hosea, Zechariah and Malachi.[15]

There are at least eight direct quotations by Christ from the Psalms (Matt. 21:16, 42; 22:44; 27:46; Mark 15:34; Luke 23:46; John 13:18; 10:34).

The extent of Christ's use of the Old Testament is not only seen from these direct references but also in the many indirect references which He makes. He refers to such individuals as Adam, Abel, Noah, Abraham, Lot, Isaac, Jacob, Moses, David, Solomon, Elijah, Elisha, Naaman, Jonah and Zacharias by name. Also, He addresses members of the angelic order (Matt. 4:10; 24:31). Geographical locations and historical events are confirmed by Him. In addition there are numerous references to institutions common in the Old Testament.

His Methods of Interpretation and Application in the Use of Scripture

The Jewish method of interpretation at the time of Christ

The predominant method of interpretation of those contemporary with Christ was the literal method. Horne states: "Although the Sanhedrin and the hearers of Jesus often ap-

[15] Isaiah is quoted in Matthew 13:13-15; 15:8, 9; Mark 4:11; 8:6, 7 and Luke 4:18, 19; 8:10; 22:37. Jeremiah is quoted in Matthew 21:13; Mark 11:17 and Luke 19:46. Hosea is quoted in Matthew 9:13; 12:7. Zechariah is quoted in Mark 14:27. Malachi is quoted in Matthew 11:10 and Luke 7:27.

pealed to the Old Testament, yet they give no indication of the allegorical interpretation; even Josephus has nothing of it. The Platonic Jews of Egypt began in the first century, in imitation of the heathen Greeks, to interpret the Old Testament allegorically. Philo of Alexandria was distinguished among those Jews who practiced this method; and he defends it as something new and before unheard of, and for that reason opposed by the other Jews. Jesus was not, therefore, in a situation in which he was compelled to comply with a prevailing custom of allegorical interpretation; for this method did not prevail at the time among the Jews, certainly not in Palestine, where Jesus taught."[16]

It must be granted that the literalism of the scribes and Pharisees was decadent and that they had warped Scripture and distorted its true meaning. The Jews of Christ's day degraded the literal interpretation of Scripture. They exalted the letter to such an extent that the true sense was lost.

The important thing is that literalism was the accepted method during the time of Christ. Granted that the method was misused this does not mean the method could not be used properly nor that it was not a proper method. There was nothing wrong with the literal method of interpretation. The Jews had simply misused and misapplied it.

Christ's method of interpretation

Christ has nowhere given a system of interpretation. However, the interpretative principles which He employed may be discovered from His teaching. A study of some of the actual interpretations which He made reveals the literal method which He used. He always interpreted Scripture with an understanding of the whole, of particular books and of parts of books. His interpretation was always in accord with the grammatical and historical meaning. He understood and appreciated the meaning intended by the writers according to the laws of grammar and rhetoric. The Saviour never perverted, distorted or misused any portion of the Word as His followers have so often done.

---

[16] Thomas Hartwell Horne, *An Introduction to the Critical Study and Knowledge of the Holy Scriptures* (London: Longman, Brown, Green and Longmans, 1859), I, 324.

Contrasted with the method of His opponents: The Lord often scorned and denounced His opponents for their faulty interpretations of Scripture. To the Sadducees He said: ". . . Is it not for this cause that ye err, that ye know not the scriptures, nor the power of God?" (Mark 12:24). The problem was not that they had not read the Scripture or did not have an intellectual acquaintance with it, but rather that they had missed its meaning by clouding it with their additions.

Failure of a correct interpretation naturally led to neglect. To the opponents of the Sadducees Jesus said: "Woe unto you scribes and Pharisees, hypocrites! for ye tithe mint and anise and cummin and have left undone the weightier matters of the law . . ." (Matt. 23:23).

Again, to the scribes Christ scathingly said: "Ye leave the commandment, and hold fast the tradition of men. And he said unto them, Full well do ye reject the commandment of God, that ye may keep your tradition" (Mark 7:8-9). "The rabbis would quote a passage and then say: 'This is the Scripture, the Word. Now I have heard Rabbi A saying he had heard from his master, Rabbi B, that Rabbi C had said that this Scripture stated thus and so.' This was their way; they relied on tradition, and the tradition was attached to the very words of the Bible . . . . It is quite different with Jesus. He says: 'I say unto you.' "[17]

Christ's rejection of the authority of Pharisaic tradition is nowhere seen more clearly than in His Sermon on the Mount (Matt. 5:17-47). This, His most formal and extended exposition of Scripture, reveals both His rejection of the tradition of the elders and His acceptance and interpretation of the law.

The purpose of treating this section of Christ's Sermon is not to expound His teaching regarding murder, adultery, divorce, oaths, non-resistance or the law of love but rather to seek to discover the method which He employed in interpreting the Scripture in contrast to the method used by the elders.

Six times Christ says with slight variation in form: "Ye have heard that it was said by them of old time . . . but I say unto you" (Matt. 5:21-43). Through these statements He

---

[17] Ernst von Dobschutz, "The Attitude of Jesus and St. Paul Toward the Bible," *The Bible Magazine*, II (July, 1914), 622.

gave a true account of those portions of the law which were involved.

Some have taken these formulas as proof that Christ was correcting the law of Moses rather than interpreting it. Those who do, take the phrase "by them of old time" as referring just to the law of Moses. That this is an incorrect and untenable position is proven by the following considerations.

First, the context of the passage forbids such an interpretation. In verses 17 through 19 Christ has summarized the relationship of Himself and His teaching to the law. He has unequivocally claimed to be the one who came to fulfil the Law and the Prophets, not to destroy them (5:17). Furthermore, He emphatically states that the whole law in its entirety is as certain of fulfillment as the certainty of the endurance of heaven and earth (5:18). Before He interprets He makes it clear that what He is going to teach is in absolute harmony with the Old Testament. According to His own testimony He came to fulfil, because not one jot or tittle shall pass from the law until all is accomplished. He did not come to destroy or make void even the smallest portion of the teaching of the Law or the Prophets. According to His estimate what may appear to be the least commandment is of equal authority with what may be considered the greatest (5:19).

Finally, as far as the context is concerned, verse 20 militates against the idea that Christ was correcting or abrogating the law. Here He proposes that His teaching is in contradiction to the teaching of the scribes and Pharisees. The Pharisees and scribes were considered holy people; yet the Lord is here teaching that because of their misunderstanding and misinterpretation of the law they were sorely lacking in true righteousness and holiness. This observation of the Lord lends strong support to the fact that Pharisaical and scribal additions to the law existed which He is about to reject. The righteousness which must exceed that possessed by the scribes and Pharisees He defines in the antitheses of 5:21-48.

Second, the formula He uses ("Ye have heard that it was said") to introduce the laws makes it clear that He is not referring merely to the law of Moses. Linguistically, the phrase τοῖς ἀρχαίοις may be variously translated and only the context can decide its meaning. "τοῖς ἀρχαίοις might mean: in ancient *times, to* the ancients, or *by* the ancients. The second is in accord with N.T. usage. . . ."[18] The Lord does not say "You have read in the law of Moses" or "It was written and you have read." He does say "You have heard." Thus, He is showing the true teaching of the law over against what was read to the people in the synagogues in addition to the law and as an explanation of it.

Third, the statement "I say unto you" demonstrates His authority to interpret the authoritative revelation of God of which none shall pass away till all is accomplished. He is not setting aside the law of Moses in any sense. "He is saying, rather, 'I am interpreting to you the law of Moses, and it is my interpretation that is true and not that of the Pharisees and scribes.' . . . 'I who am speaking to you am the very One who was responsible for the law of Moses; it was I who gave it to Moses, and it is I alone, therefore, who can truly interpret it.' "[19]

Thus Christ interpreted the very words of Scripture without relying on any admixture of human tradition. His whole argument is to the effect that the Pharisees and scribes in their attempt to obey the letter had missed the spirit. His interpretations of the six laws to which He refers shows that the heart of man is the source of sinful actions. These laws set forth the spiritual requirements of inward righteousness which are demanded by God whenever the kingdom is offered. They are in stunning contrast to external righteousnesses of the Pharisees.

Scripture interpreted by Scripture: A few illustrations of this principle of interpretation from Christ's teaching will suffice. What is meant by this principle is that the scope and significance of one passage is brought out by its relation to other passages. When the Lord used Moses' law of divorce to show that it was a temporary arrangement instituted because of the hardness of the human heart He used this method of interpretation (cf. Matt. 19:3-8 and Deut. 24:1).

Often the Lord bade the Pharisees and scribes to return to school and learn to interpret the letter of individual Scriptures in light of the spirit which pervaded the whole. His

[18] Alexander Balmain Bruce, "The Synoptic Gospels," *The Expositor's Greek Testament*, ed. W. Robertson Nicoll (Grand Rapids: Wm. B. Eerdmans Publishing Company, 1951), I, 106.

[19] D. Martyn Lloyd-Jones, *Studies in the Sermon on the Mount* (Grand Rapids: Wm. B. Eerdmans Publishing Company, 1959), I, 213-14.

reference to Hosea 6:6 in Matthew 12:3-7 is illustrative of the fact that God's revelation in the Old Testament is significantly understood in the New. If the Jews of His day would have understood God's words "I desire mercy and not sacrifice" (Hos. 6:6) they would not have been so quick to condemn the guiltless (Matt. 12:4-7). On another occasion Christ turned their attention to the same text to remind them that His offer of the kingdom was for sinners, not the self-righteous.

Also, in the temptation account Christ answered Satan's challenging reference to Psalm 91:11, 12 by referring him to a companion passage in Deuteronomy 6:16 (Matt. 4:6, 7). Both passages were equally true but the one sets boundaries to the interpretation of the other. God does protect and care for His own but they are not to foolishly presume upon His promise.

Interpretation before application: There is not one single instance where Christ uses Scripture in a distorted and far-fetched way. Frequently, His interpretation is accompanied by His application to life situations. A formal interpretation is not always stated by Christ in His application but no application is ever made which does violence to the meaning of the historical-grammatical construction. Frequently, the Saviour interpreted a text by applying it to some concrete case. He was ever conscious of the needs of men and interpreted and applied Scripture with that in view.

The multiplicity of uses which Christ makes of the Scriptures never reveals anything but an interpretation based upon the historical-grammatical sense of Scripture.

Christ's method of application

As was stated earlier Christ's application of Scripture is always based on a proper interpretation and the two are always seen together. His method of application may be studied as it concerns Himself and as it concerns others.

In relation to Himself: The principal passage to be used in this connection which illustrates the point under consideration is Matthew 4:1-11. This passage will receive attention again in another connection; here it will serve to demonstrate how the Saviour applied Scripture to Himself.

In this, the very first recorded instance of His quotation of Scripture, He makes application of three distinct passages of Scripture to His own needs. Each of the three avenues of temptation centered in His personal needs. He was hungry, He did want to proclaim His deity and He did need to demonstrate His kingship.

Each of the avenues of temptation are resisted and answered by a quotation from Deuteronomy prefaced by "it stands written." There are three outstanding principles used by Christ in each of His references to the passages in Deuteronomy (Deut. 8:3; 6:16; 6:13). These principles give insight into His method of application in relation to Himself.

First, a study of the contexts of the passages quoted reveals a parallel between the historical circumstances and the circumstances in which Christ found Himself. Israel was being tested in the wilderness, as was Christ, to show the importance of dependence on God (Matt. 4:3; cf. Deut. 8:3). Too, Israel had made a test case for God and that is precisely what Satan wanted Christ to do (Matt. 4:6; cf. Deut. 6:16). The third avenue of temptation also finds its parallel in the Old Testament. Israel was in peril of seeking the favor and protection of a god other than Jehovah. This is precisely what Satan wanted Christ to do—to find protection in him rather than in Jehovah.

Second, by His application of the Deuteronomy passages Christ reveals His own relation to the nation Israel. He sees a parallel between His case and the case of those to whom Moses wrote. The very fact that He so used Scripture shows that while Scripture was written to meet the immediate needs of the people to whom it was originally addressed, it also is applicable to the circumstances of the lives of others.

Third, Christ does not force the language or impose a foreign sense into the words of Moses. The original and proper significance of the words is not distorted or lost in the Lord's usage. The words meant for Him what they meant to those to whom they were originally addressed. He never ignores the meaning to make an application. Rather, the application results strictly from the meaning. Proof of this principle is in this very passage. Satan attempted to misuse the Scripture in his quotation (Matt. 4:6) by failing to see the unity of Scripture. Christ quickly reminds him that it also stands written, "Thou shalt not make trial of the Lord thy God" (Matt. 4:7). "When Satan misuses Scripture by mutilating a quotation from Psalm 91:11-12, with a view to making the life-giving Word of God become mortal to Christ and to changing good food into poison, it is once again with Scripture that Christ repulses such insinuations."[20]

In relation to others: Christ applied the Scriptures in His dealing with others in the same way in which He applied them to Himself. Though there is only one true interpretation of Scripture there are many applications and Christ's use of Scripture illustrates this. He made Scripture applicable to the needs of people. Several instances of His application will suffice to illustrate the point.

When the Lord wanted to warn men of the danger of preoccupation with things of this life and the certainty of coming judgment He reminded them of Noah's day (Luke 17:27). Likewise, to warn against moral and spiritual decline ". . . He recalls to their memories the shortest biography in the world, encompassed in the Old Testament within the limits of a single sentence (Gen. 19:26) and retold by Himself in three penetrating words 'Remember Lot's wife' (Luke 17:32."[21]

Jeremiah's description of the temple as a "den of robbers" (Jer. 7:11) was as applicable to the temple of Jesus' day (Matt. 12:13). For Christ the moral necessity of inward righteousness was no different in His day than in Moses' day. He summarizes His teaching of moral duty by quoting Deuteronomy 6:4, 5 and Leviticus 19:18 (Matt. 22:37-40).

The two on the road to Emmaus after the resurrection certainly had real needs and Christ met those needs not merely by applying one or two passages of Scripture for them but by causing them to understand His exposition and application of the law of Moses, the Prophets and the Psalms (Luke 24:44).

Though a multitude of references might be brought forth to further amplify the fact that Christ applied Scripture to the needs of men, the above instances will suffice to illustrate the point. Whenever He makes an application He does so on

---

[20] Pierre Ch. Marcel, "Our Lord's Use of Scripture," *Revelation and the Bible*, ed. Carl F. H. Henry (Grand Rapids: Baker Book House, 1958), p. 130.

[21] R. V. G. Tasker, *The Old Testament in the New Testament* (Grand Rapids: Wm. B. Eerdmans Publishing Co., 1963), pp. 24-25.

the basis of the historical-grammatical meaning and the appropriateness of the truth to present circumstances. Thus, this area of the Master's teaching agrees with all the others in that He demonstrated His faith in Scripture as that which is the rule of faith and practice for all under all circumstances and in every age.

From this general study of Christ's use of Scripture it has been demonstrated that He recognized it as the authoritative revelation of God. Every aspect of His usage substantiates His acceptance of it and complete reliance upon its authority. His references to the Old Testament are not incidental and isolated. As a concluding statement regarding Christ's entire use of the Scripture the statement of D. Martyn Lloyd-Jones well summarizes this chapter: "He puts His seal of authority, His *imprimatur,* upon the whole of the Old Testament canon, the whole of the law and the prophets. . . . He believed it all and not only certain parts of it! He quoted almost every part of it. To the Lord Jesus Christ the Old Testament was the Word of God; it was Scripture; it was something absolutely unique and apart; it had authority which nothing else has ever possessed nor can possess."[22]

---

[22] Lloyd-Jones, *op. cit.,* p. 187.

CHAPTER II

THE ORIGIN OF SCRIPTURE IN THE SAVIOUR'S TEACHING

The evidence is overwhelming. The Saviour used the Scriptures often, for many purposes and under differing circumstances; yet He always ascribed to them the same loyalty and devotion as the final appeal in all matters upon which they pronounced.

Our purpose now will be to consider Christ's specific teaching of the source or origin of Scripture. From whence have these Scriptures come which He used so freely? Certainly, His use of Scripture indicates that He accepted it as that which came from God. However, He made specific pronouncement indicating His own view of the origin or revelation of Scripture. The concepts of revelation and inspiration are difficult to distinguish in Christ's teaching. These two concepts are not synonymous though they are similar. Revelation has to do with the impartation of truth while inspiration, strictly speaking, has to do with the recording of that truth.

The two doctrines are often confused especially by liberal theologians. They often fail to distinguish between the fact that God has revealed Himself and the resultant written product of that revelation. There is a converging point in revelation and inspiration and in Christ's teaching it is sometimes difficult to separate the one from the other.

The present purpose, however, is to discover Christ's teaching of the source of Scripture.

THE SOURCE OF REVELATION

Theologically, the term *revelation* may be defined as the divine act of communicating to man what otherwise man would not know and could not know but must come to know to be rightly related to God. While the revelation of God is not exclusively confined to Scripture Christ makes no reference to any other medium. He never questioned the divine source of Scripture. For Him what God spoke was Scripture and Scripture is what God spoke. He used the terms "scripture" and "word of God" interchangeably (John 10:34-35).

First, we want to cite evidence from general considerations and then evidence from specific passages which reveal Christ's teaching of the divine origin of Scripture. It will also be of interest to discover the means by which the revelation was given and the character and purpose of the revelation.

Proof from general considerations

Almost every reference which Christ makes to the Old Testament whether it is direct or indirect, explicit or implicit, will substantiate the thesis that He regarded Scripture as from God.

Names and titles: The names and titles which Christ used to designate Holy Writ indicate His belief in its divine origin. Such titles as "Scripture," and "Word of God" imply clearly the divine source and authority of the Old Testament. "It will be seen in each of the three titles referred to—the Word, the Scripture and the Law—tribute is paid to the divine origin and authority of the Book. By 'the Word' we are given to understand that Jesus accepted it as a communication from God. In his use of the term 'Scripture' we perceive that he approved it, in its written form, as intended, for common use. And when he called it 'The Law' he emphasized its authority as a trustworthy rule of life."[1] The names and titles Christ used when referring to Scripture were familiar designations to the Jewish mind and vocabulary. However, they were not terms which were used carelessly. They were reserved exclusively for the sacred canon of Scripture and it is in this sense which Christ used them.

Christ's declaration in John 10:34-35 is illustrative of His equating of the term "scripture" with other terms. He refers to Scripture, Law and the Word of God as one and the same. Commenting on Christ's usage in this passage Warfield writes: "When Jesus adduces this passage then, as written in the 'law' of the Jews, He does it, not because it

[1] David James Burrell, *The Teaching of Jesus Concerning the Scriptures* (New York: American Tract Society, 1904), p. 120.

stands in this psalm, but it is a part of Scripture at large. In other words, He here ascribes legal authority to the entirety of Scripture in accordance with a conception common enough among the Jews (cf. Jn. 12:34), and finding expression in the New Testament occasionally, both on the lips of Jesus Himself, and in the writing of the apostles."[2]

Acceptance of current Jewish belief: Combined with Christ's extended use of Scripture discussed in the previous chapter is the additional argument that He never once questioned the prevailing Jewish belief in the divine origin of Scripture. His extensive use of Scripture can only be accounted for on the basis of His trust in its divine source unless He be deprived of the intelligence and integrity which His person demands. That the Jews of Christ's day accepted the Old Testament as the divine deposit of truth is a generally accepted fact. They never argued with Him and He never argued with them on this point. In spite of all His criticisms of their views on other things He never debated with them over the divine origination of their Scriptures. This was one of their cherished possessions. "The use of this term in the N. T. was an inheritance, not an invention. The idea of a 'canon' of 'Sacred Scriptures' (and with the idea the thing) was handed down to Christianity from Judaism."[3]

Paul voiced the Jewish sentiment when he said that to Israel belongs "the covenants" and "the giving of the law and the promises" (Rom. 9:4). "In no nation was the universal belief of the ancient world in the intercourse between heaven and earth so deeply rooted as among the Jews. Their writings, composed subsequently to the completion of the Old Testament, afford the most decisive proof of their ascribing Inspiration to the authors of the several parts; and leave no doubt as to their conviction that the collection of Sacred Books was defined under the Divine guidance and closed at the Divine command."[4]

---

[2] Benjamin Breckinridge Warfield, *The Inspiration and Authority of the Bible* (Philadelphia: The Presbyterian and Reformed Publishing Company, 1948), pp. 138-39.

[3] Benjamin Breckinridge Warfield, "Scripture," *A Dictionary of Christ and the Gospels*, ed. James Hastings (New York: Charles Scribner's Sons, 1912), II, 584.

[4] William Lee, *The Inspiration of Scripture* (New York: Robert Carter and Brothers, 1857), p. 61.

It is this high view of Scripture current among the Jews that Christ accepted and taught. He never accepted the additions and false interpretations which the Jews placed upon the Old Testament. Their views tended to divorce the divine nature and authority of the Scriptures from the human authors. Their distorted view also abstracted the Scripture from the object of its witness—Jesus Christ. Because of their rejection of the Christ of the Scriptures the words which they read had been deprived of divine power.

According to Christ's testimony it was not the Jewish belief in the divine origin of Scripture that was wrong but their refusal to accept the one of whom the Holy Spirit spoke in the Old Testament.

Acceptance of the miraculous in history: It may be inferred from Christ's repeated references to historical events and happenings, which were either the evidence of some spectacular display of God's power or were of a miraculous nature, that the Old Testament came from God. His references to such events and episodes include creation (Matt. 19:4), the flood (Matt. 24:37-39), the burning bush (Mark 12:26), the supply of manna (John 6:32), the serpent in the wilderness (John 6:14), the famine of Elijah's day (Luke 4:25) and the cleansing of Naaman the leper (Luke 4:27). Only a divine book would record such divine undertakings. The fact that Christ recognized these supernatural undertakings as they were recorded in the Old Testament indicates His acceptance of its divine nature. These were not natural phenomena and Christ did not treat them as such.

Constant appeal to Scripture: His constant appeal to the Old Testament both for Himself and for others lends support to the fact of His belief in its supernatural origin. He not only appealed to it in the presence of the multitudes but also when He was alone. He appealed to it with the same dependence while on the cross and after His resurrection as He had throughout His life's ministry. The Old Testament was His constant recourse and bulwark of defense. This fact ought to indicate His belief in its divine origin, for on what else would or could the Son of God depend than the very Word of God?

Recognition of prophetic element in Scripture: Finally, it may be observed that Christ's recognition of the prophetic element in Scripture argues for His confidence in its divine origin. The phrase "that it might be fulfilled" or its equivalents was frequently spoken by Christ implying that either the Old Testament already received fulfillment or was to be fulfilled in the future. These statements which imply a prophetic element in Scripture certainly reveal the diversity of Scripture. No man, unaided by the Spirit, can tell what is hidden in the future.

Only what God has spoken could always be depended upon as certain and sure of fulfillment. Christ emphasized that the God from whom the Scripture came is the God who guaranteed its accuracy.

Proof from specific passages

Beyond the general considerations cited above implying Christ's teaching of the divine origin of Scripture there are several specific passages where Christ teaches this fact. These references teach in the strongest language possible that the Scriptures originated with God. Their source is found in Him. Some of these passages have been cited earlier to illustrate other points and some of them will of necessity be used again when dealing with Christ's concept of inspiration.

Matthew 22:31-32: The argument which the Sadducees raised regarding the resurrection was answered by Christ's quotation of the words of Moses in Exodus 3:6. "But as touching the resurrection of the dead, have ye not read that which was spoken unto you by God, saying, I am the God of Abraham, and the God of Isaac, and the God of Jacob? God is not the God of the dead but of the living" (Matt. 22:31-32). His answer caused great astonishment among the multitudes (Matt. 22:31-32; Mark 12:26). The important fact in these words of Christ, for the present consideration, is that Christ prefaced His quotation of Moses' words by saying it was spoken unto them "by God." The Lord does not answer the question of the Sadducees by citing the strong testimony of the prophets concerning the resurrection, which He could have done (Isa. 26:19; Ezek. 37:1-14; Dan. 12:2). Rather, He turns to the Mosaic source from which their difficulty had been raised. He declares to them, concerning books with which they were perfectly familiar both as to authorship and content, that what Moses had written God had said. Their objection began on the basis of what Moses had said. Christ's reply proceeds on the basis of what God had said, which things Moses had received and recorded.

Matthew 15:3-6: The Pharisees and scribes asked Jesus why His disciples did not keep the tradition of the elders since they ate with unwashed hands. Christ's answer astounded them because He in reply accused them of transgressing "the commandment of God" and making void "the word of God" because they had failed to remember that what Moses recorded in Exodus 20:12 and Deuteronomy 5:16, God had said (Matt. 15:3-6; Mark 7:8-13). Christ here claims the divine origin of the law. The commandment of God, the word or law of God was the revelation of God to man. Alford recognizes the phrase "the commandment of God" as ". . . a remarkable testimony from our Lord to the divine origin of the Mosaic law: not merely of the Decalogue, as such, for the second command quoted is not in the Decalogue, and it is to be observed that where the text has ὁ ϑέος ἐντείλατο, Mark (7:10) has Μωυσῆς εἶπεν."[5]

Matthew 19:4-5: Here the Saviour advances a line of argument similar to that in Matthew 15. "And he answered and said, Have ye not read, that he who made them from the beginning made them male and female, and said For this cause shall a man leave his father and mother, and shall cleave to his wife; and the two shall become one flesh?" (Matt. 19:4-5).

The question before the Lord concerned the matter of divorce. Our present concern is not to expound Christ's teaching on divorce but with the fact that Christ here attributed to God what actually was spoken and recorded by Moses. He not only acknowledged the historical fact of creation but He also attributes to God what was actually said by the law-giver.

John 10:35: Here a portion of the Psalms is called "the word of God" by Christ (John 10:35; cf. Ps. 82:6). The inviolability of the Scripture which Christ claims by the words "the scripture cannot be broken" is promised upon the fact that it was of divine origin and thus "the word of God."

Other passages could be cited where Christ clearly recognized the divine source of Scripture. These should be sufficient, however, to demonstrate the validity of the proposition that Christ traced the origin of Scripture beyond man and his imaginations to God Himself.

---

[5] Henry Alford, *The Greek Testament* (Chicago: Moody Press, 1958), I, II, 162.

The Means of the Revelation

The media by which God has revealed Himself in Scripture are included in Christ's teaching. The fact has been established that God has made Himself and His will known. It remains to be seen how and through what means He accomplished this revelatory act. Christ's teaching does not encompass all the modalities of revelation. Those which He has seen fit to include are the most inclusive and all-encompassing in their revelation of God.

Revelation in Christ

The Apostle John declared: "No man hath seen God at any time; the only begotten Son, who is in the bosom of the Father, he hath declared him" (John 1:18). Christ Himself clearly sought to teach His disciples this same truth (cf. John 14:9, 24; 17:6, 8, 14; Matt. 11:27).

Christ constitutes the apex of God's revelation to man both qualitatively and chronologically. He is the ultimate in manifestation of God to man. This is the united testimony of Peter (2 Pet. 1:19), the Gospel writers (Matt. 7:28-29; John 1:18), Paul (Col. 1:15) and the writer to the Hebrews (Heb. 1:1-2). It is also Christ's view of Himself: "I have yet many things to say unto you but ye cannot bear them now" (John 16:12). Here Christ is claiming to be both the originator and the mode of revelation, the one from whom revelation comes and the one who gives revelation.

There is a note of finality about Christ as the revelation of God. The revelation of God in His person is not a continuous process. It was completed at the incarnation (John 1:18; 14:9; Heb. 1:2) and the completed revelation of God in Christ is deposited in the Scriptures.

Before coming to Christ's teaching of the revelation of God to man in words it is necessary to say a word about His references to revelatory events in the Old Testament. These revelatory events already listed above include such things as creation, the flood, the burning bush, the supply of manna, the serpent in the wilderness, the famine of Elijah's day and the cleansing of Naaman the leper. From Christ's reference to these events it may be inferred that He was implying their revelatory nature. However, the emphasis which Christ places upon the very words of God makes it clear that revelation through acts is inadequate and unintelligible apart from words. Christ's emphasis is upon revelation in words, the words of God to man.

Revelation to men

On four different occasions the Lord referred His hearers to the Scripture by naming the human writers of the revelation of God. Thus, He taught that though the Scriptures were of divine origin they were made known to men and recorded by men.

Moses: Reference is made by Christ to Moses many times either directly or indirectly. Each time a reference is made, the authoritative nature of his writings is implied if not clearly stated (Matt. 8:4; Mark 12:26; John 5:45-46). Christ assigns the authorship of the Pentateuch to Moses at least ten times and each time He does He flatly contradicts the destructive higher critics (Matt. 19:7, 8; 23:2; Mark 10:3; Luke 16:29, 31; 24:27; John 5:45, 46; 7:19, 23). In this as in many other areas it is either Christ or the critics. It cannot be both.

David: Psalm 110 as the revelation of God is said to be written by David (Matt. 22:43-44; Mark 12:36; Luke 20:42). In this reference to David, Christ is not only claiming him as the human penman but also the one through whom the Spirit spoke. From Christ's statement it is crystal clear that He is saying the Spirit was the divine author and David the human writer of Psalm 110.

Through His infallible observation the Lord is thus agreeing with David's own deathbed testimony: "The Spirit of Jehovah spake by me, and his word was upon my tongue" (2 Sam. 23:2). With these two recorded testimonies Peter through the promised ministry of the Spirit declared the same truth when he said ". . . the scripture should be fulfilled, which the Holy Spirit spake before by the mouth of David . . ." (Acts 1:16).

Isaiah: According to Christ this prophet was the writer of the book which bears his name. The spiritual insensitivity of the religious He associates with the prophecy of Isaiah (Matt. 13:14-15; cf. Isa. 6:9, 10). While denouncing the scribes and Pharisees for their hypocricy the Saviour quotes from this prophet (Matt. 15:7-9; cf. Isa. 29:13). Christ's endorsement of Isaiah as the human penman of the revelation of God may also be inferred from the account of His reading in the synagogue (Luke 4:17-19). Without mentioning the prophet's name, Christ clearly shows His endorsement of the writings of Isaiah by reading with acceptance that which was unquestionably assigned to Isaiah.

Christ did not always name the prophet Isaiah when using portions of his writings. An illustration of this is found in John 6:45, "And it is written in the prophets, And they shall all be taught of God." This is either reference to Iśaiah 54:13 or possibly Jeremiah 31:34. Perhaps the use of the plural "prophets" indicates that more than one prophecy is referred to. It certainly implies that He regarded all this group of writings as one book and that He was familiar with all the books in the group.

Daniel: Christ acclaimed Daniel as the one who wrote of the "abomination of desolation" (Matt. 24:15; Mark 13:14; cf. Dan. 9:27). He specifically names Daniel and states that he wrote so that "whoso readeth" could understand. There seems to be an emphasis on the recorded aspect of the message. Also, the context of Christ's reference implies He and Daniel were prophets and what they prophesy will stand or fall together. The one spoken of is viewed as historical a personage as the one speaking. This prophet's writings are stamped with divine authority. The Saviour makes what Daniel said His very own. He adds to it His own authority guaranteeing its fulfillment.

The significance of the references: Christ's mention of these human authors is significant for three reasons.

First, their mention illustrates the fact that the incomprehensible God condescended to make Himself and His will known to sinful man. Christ does not engage in discussion of the media by which God revealed Himself to man such as dreams, visions, theophanies and angels. He only acknowledges that God called into service human beings for His holy task. These were sinful men. Think of the sin of David with Bathsheba (2 Sam. 11, 12). Yet these were men through whom God the Spirit spoke and whom He protected from all error.

Second, significantly enough, the writings of these men encompass the three divisions of the Scriptures recognized by the Jews of Christ's time. Thus Christ recognized the human counterpart of the divine revelation in the entire Old Testament, for it existed as a unit and to acknowledge one part was to acknowledge all parts.

Third, they are important because of the manner in which Christ treats them. It is indeed significant that He mentions only four human writers as authors. Especially is this true since He made such an abundant use of the Old Testament. Other men are named but not other authors of Scripture. Even in the cases of these which He does identify as writers He gives no intimation that the writers were the source of authority; in fact, the reverse is true. He emphasizes not the authority of the men but what they wrote. There is not a single instance where Christ ever alluded to the inspiration of authors. However, on the other hand, neither does He ever give so much as a hint that they were in error as recipients and recorders of God's revelation. It is indeed an amazing thing that God would so use the men whom He created to be the vehicles through whom He would reveal Himself. This is true especially since they were sinful men.

The problem of accommodation with these men: A word is in order at this point concerning the claim of some that Christ in so referring to the Old Testament, and these four authors in particular, was merely accommodating Himself to the prevailing belief about them. It is supposed that His appeal to the Old Testament was not because He accepted its authority but because He knew His hearers did and He thus hoped to gain a quicker acceptance for His own teaching by claiming agreement with them. This hypothesis is impossible in light of the following considerations.

The integrity and thus the deity of Christ is impugned by such a view. If their view was wrong and He in honesty did not share it, He lived and taught a lie by making them believe He did. "If we reject His attitude to the Old Testament, we are saying in effect that He founded Christianity on a fallacy. And if we say He was wrong here, we really imply that He was wrong everywhere; for His view of the nature and authority of the Old Testament underlies all He said and did."[6]

Then there is also the fact that in each of the instances where He refers to the men listed above as authors the entire validity of His argument rests upon His own acceptance of that which He is teaching. This is illustrated clearly in the case of David. The fact that He claimed to be the stone rejected by Israel (Mark 12:10) and was the one who could answer the questions of the scribes and Pharisees with such baffling recourse to the authority of Scripture (Mark 12:13-34) is dependent upon His superiority to David and His unique lordship spoken of by David himself in Psalm 110 (Mark 12:35). It might have been legitimate for Christ to argue on the assumption that since *they* believed David to be the author and Messiah to be his son, therefore He could ask them how it was that David called the Messiah his Lord if He was to be his son. "But when a person employs this mode of reasoning he should say so, and should not profess to reason on other grounds. Our Lord does not say so, and does profess to reason on other grounds; for he affirms for himself his belief that David wrote the Psalm . . . guided by the Spirit of inspiration, and foreseeing that the Messiah should be both his Lord and his son."[7]

This view of accommodation in relation to these authors is impossible also because it does not explain His usage of Scripture elsewhere. For example, in the Sermon on the Mount He takes great care to separate the divine law from the misconceptions and erroneous deductions of scribal tradition. There seems to be no hesitation on His part to scathingly denounce His contemporaries on many points. He does not hesitate in His Sermon to undermine current belief. He constantly denounced Pharisaic traditionalism. He was even prepared to face the cross for defying misconceptions of His Messiahship.

What was true in the Sermon on the Mount is equally true in His temptation experience. Here He was alone with Satan.

---

[6] J. I. Packer, *"Fundamentalism" and the Word of God* (Grand Rapids: Wm. B. Eerdmans Publishing Co., 1960), p. 60.

[7] Franklin Johnson, *The Quotations of the New Testament from the Old Considered in the Light of General Literature* (Philadelphia: American Baptist Publication Society, 1896), pp. 343-44.

There was no need to accommodate Himself to any current Jewish misconceptions, for the crowd of both friends and foes was absent.

The facts associated with Christ's entire use of Scripture, therefore, militate against any concept of accommodation on His part with regard to the books and human writers which He names.

Revelation in words

This fact which is so often rejected by men was taught by the Lord. He did not hesitate to declare that God *sometimes* gave the precise words to the human writers of Scripture. Christ does not teach that God dictated every word of Scripture to the authors, else the entire Scriptures would be the product of verbal dictation which they are not. His general teaching would indicate that what men wrote in Scripture was of divine origination and was what God the revealer wanted revealed and written. Nevertheless, Christ taught that in some instances God communicated His truth to man in dictated words.

This is clearly taught in Mark 12:26: ". . . God spake unto him, saying, I am the God of Abraham, and the God of Isaac, and the God of Jacob." The reference is to Exodus 3:6 where it is equally clear that God was doing the revealing, the speaking to Moses, and Moses merely recorded what God said. Matthew also declares these words of Moses to be the words of God in his parallel account (Matt. 22:31).

These two companion passages teach two profound truths. They teach the revelation of God in words and therefore the inspiration of those words, a point to be considered subsequently. It may be argued that the thrust of the passages is not on the words which God is reputed to have spoken but on the truth that God is at no time the God of the dead but of the living. This is true and the issue with the Sadducees was the resurrection. The impact and forcefulness of Christ's reply, however, is that His answer was the answer of the words of God to Moses. This is what astonished the multitudes and angered the Pharisees (Matt. 22:23-34).

Christ's words in Matthew 15:4 indicate that God dictated words to Moses in the giving of the ten commandments. "For

God said, Honor thy father and thy mother, and, He that speaketh evil of father or mother, let him die the death" (Matt. 15:4; cf. Ex. 20:12; Deut. 5:16; Ex. 21:17; Lev. 20:9). These passages are forceful and meaningful. They do more than prove that the Old Testament merely expressed the mind of God in some general way. They teach more than a general endorsement by Christ of the Scriptures. Emphatically, they declare the Saviour's view of the divine origin of Scripture.

The Character of the Revelation

Thus far it has been demonstrated from general considerations and specific passages that Christ viewed Scripture as the revelation of God. Evidence has been presented to show the way and means by which that revelation was given. It remains to be seen from the teaching of Christ how He characterized this revelation from God.

Revelation as progressive and complete

The many instances in which Christ speaks of the Scripture, as fulfilled or to be fulfilled, teach that the divinely originated revelation of God was given progressively to men and completely in Him. The fact that Scripture must be fulfilled indicates a progressive and culminating process whereby God will bring to pass that which He promised.

A clear reference by Christ to the progressive nature of the revelation is seen in His words: "The law and the prophets were until John" (Luke 16:16). Burrell observes: ". . . 'by the law and the prophets' he meant the Scriptures . . . and by saying that they 'were until John' he could only mean that they had been divinely intended as a trustworthy guide in all things looking forward and leading up to the gospel dispensation. In so far as they were prophetic or symbolical they were proven true by their perfect fulfillment in that dispensation as 'the kingdom of God.' "[8]

Christ allows for further revelation based upon His own personal revealing and revelation in the Upper Room Discourse. Speaking of the coming of the Holy Spirit He said, ". . . he shall teach you all things, and bring to your remem-

[8] Burrell, *op. cit.*, p. 68.

brance all that I said unto you" (John 14:26). Again, "Howbeit when he, the Spirit of truth, is come, he shall guide you into all the truth" (John 16:13). The Saviour thus not only allowed for more truth but made it clear that truth to be given subsequent to His departure was to be based upon the revelation He had already given (John 16:13, 14).

That Christ taught the completeness and finality of the revelation of God in Himself is proven by His consistent testimony that He came to fulfill the law (e.g., Matt. 5:17, 18). His deeds as well as His didactic ministry lend full support to His firm belief that the special revelation of God found its culmination in Him.

Christ's fulfillment of the law involved more than an affirmation of its validity; it also meant that God had disclosed a new and final revelation in Christ. Stonehouse was correct when he said: "The profound affirmation of Matthew is that *the coming of the Messiah signifies the coming of one whose life and teaching were themselves a new epochal revelation that was the consummation of the old.*"[9]

It must not be assumed from the above discussion that Christ viewed God's earlier revelation as less truthful and less authoritative than His final revelation. His use of the early Mosaic records of the revelation of God militates against such a concept, for never once does He question the authority of any portion of Scripture. In fact He viewed the early portions of Scripture with the same confidence as the later prophetic portions. His teaching supports the progressive unfolding of God's mind and will but not the idea that earlier revelations were less authoritative. Warfield has summarized this culminating aspect of Christ's revelation in his usual clarity: "Nevertheless, though all revelation is thus summed up in Him, we should not fail to note very carefully that it would also be all sealed up in Him—so little is revelation conveyed by fact alone, without the word—had it not been thus taken by the Spirit of truth and declared unto men. The entirety of the New Testament is but the explanatory word accompanying and giving its effect to the fact of Christ. And when this fact was in all its meaning made the possession of men,

[9] Ned Bernard Stonehouse, *The Witness of Matthew and Mark to Christ* (Philadelphia: The Presbyterian Guardian, 1944), p. 198.

revelation was completed and in that sense ceased. Jesus Christ is no less the end of revelation than He is the end of the law."[10]

Revelation as law

It has already been acknowledged that Christ applied the title "law" to the Pentateuch. The term "law" was also used by Him as a general term including the whole of Scripture. Examples of this may be found in John 10:34 where He quotes Psalm 82:6 and calls it "your law." Speaking of His rejection to His disciples He said, "But this cometh to pass, that the word may be fulfilled that is written in their law, They hated me without a cause (John 15:25). This is a reference to Psalm 35:19 and 69:4 and these portions do not appear in the law division of the Old Testament. By His use of this title Christ was recognizing the binding and authoritative character of Scripture.

Revelation as truth

As Christ approached His death He acknowledged by a specific statement the Word of God as truth. He said: "Sanctify them in the truth: thy word is truth" (John 17:17). The fact that this statement comes near the end of His earthly life does not mean that He did not accept the Word as truth before. This acknowledgement comes in the section of the prayer where He prays for the disciples. No doubt they heard the words of Christ in this prayer and thus were assured that the same faith in Scripture which characterized Christ's entire life of ministry was still His. God's Word which He revealed is thus made synonymous with truth in this statement. Thus, this is a declaration that the Word of God is not only true but is itself the embodiment of truth.

Revelation as sufficient

This characteristic of God's revelation in Scripture is taught primarily by Christ's use of Scripture and His consistent attitude toward it. The fact that He used the Old Testament and applied it under every circumstance is evi-

[10] Benjamin Breckinridge Warfield, *Revelation and Inspiration* (New York: Oxford University Press, 1927), p. 28.

dence that He acknowledged it as that which could be trusted and relied upon for every circumstance of life. If He, the Son of God, resorted to the Word of God for every need of His own life certainly it may be assumed that He accepted it as sufficient also for others.

Luke's account of the words of Christ in Luke 16:31 bears testimony to His confidence in the sufficiency of Scripture: "And he said unto him, If they hear not Moses and the prophets, neither will they be persuaded, if one rise from the dead." The implication of this statement is that Moses and the prophets represented God's utmost as a guide to salvation and eternal life.

The Purpose of the Revelation

The fact has been established that in the mind and teaching of Jesus, Scripture finds its source with God. This answers the question, Where did Scripture originate? Christ also taught how the revelation of God in Scripture was made known. God made Himself known to men. At least sometimes His revelation came dictatorially in words. The climactic apex of His revelation was in Christ. The question of what the revelation was like, was taught clearly by the Lord as well. The remaining question before us is: Why was the revelation given? What purpose, in the teaching of Christ, did God have for making Himself and His will known? In somewhat incidental ways Christ reveals three basic purposes for God's revelation in Scripture.

To reveal the person of God

If the fact be accepted that Scripture came from God and that it is therefore truth—God's truth—then it is as certain as it is obvious that Scripture reveals the nature of God. Thus, according to Christ, within the Scripture there is the revelation of the person of God. What God has said in Scripture is a disclosure of Himself. Following this line of reasoning every reference which Christ makes to Scripture is a reference to some truth about the person of God, for His person is revealed unmistakably only in Scripture. Two examples of the revelation of God's person in Scripture from the teaching of Christ will be presented briefly.

God of the living: This truth was imparted to the Sadducees in reply to their question regarding the resurrection. Though this passage has been used previously for other purposes and will be used again, it clearly sets forth the mind of Christ concerning the person of God from Exodus 3:6. He said God spake unto Moses saying, ". . . I am the God of Abraham, and the God of Isaac, and the God of Jacob. He is not the God of the dead, but of the living: ye do greatly err" (Mark 12:26-27). Christ thus taught two unmistakable truths about the person of God and each one assumes the other. He taught the eternality of God by His use of the present tense "I am." He also taught, in conjunction with this, that the eternal God is thus the God of the living. The point can be argued either from the eternal God or the God of the living because to be one He had to be the other.

The point to be made here is that this revelation concerning God was unknown to the Sadducees because they did not know the Scriptures, the only place where the revelation was deposited. In those Scriptures God said "I *am*" the God of Abraham, not "I *was*." The import of the quotation is to demonstrate that God was successively the God of Abraham, Isaac and Jacob when each one was living. Yet when God spoke to Moses even though the patriarchs had long since departed, He was still their God.

God of power: The Scriptures were given to bear testimony to the power of God. In the same passage discussed above Christ accused the Sadducees of not knowing the power of God because they did not know the Scriptures of God. It may therefore be concluded that the purpose of the revelation in Scripture is to declare God's power. Failure to understand the Scriptures produced ignorance of the power of God.

The questioners had so worded and complicated their question as to make it serve as a strong *reductio ad absurdum.* Christ did not stop with the declaration of their ignorance of Scripture which produced their error but went on to explain the accompanying error which the first one caused. Quite possibly, to the surprise of the Sadducees, Christ relates God to the resurrection—the God of power.

It naturally follows if God has the power of resurrection He is all-powerful. That Scripture reveals the power of God in Christ's teaching may also be seen from Christ's reference to the creation account (Matt. 19:4-5). Christ's specific mention of such recorded revelations of God's power serves to illustrate something of the purpose of the revelation.

To reveal the purpose of God

This fact relates to the will of God in Christ's teaching. Scripture was given so that man may know the will of God for his life. Christ's emphasis was also upon the fact that the revelation of God was given to make known the will of God for the Son.

The purpose of God for men: The abundant use which Christ made of Scripture should demonstrate His belief that if men were to know the will of God for their lives they had to know the Word of God, for therein was the will of God made known. If Christ be accepted on His own claims and those of His disciples, it must be granted that His frequent recommendation of Scripture for His followers and His foes is proof that He accepted it as sufficient and as that which made known adequately the will and purpose of God.

The purpose of God for Christ: The entire life of Christ from birth to death was lived by doing the Father's will. His incarnation and birth were the subject of Scripture (Matt. 1:22-23; cf. Isa. 7:14). The flight into Egypt fulfilled Scripture (Matt. 2:13-15; cf. Hos. 11:1). Christ's days of childhood in Nazareth had been referred to by Isaiah (Matt. 2:19-23; cf. Isa. 11:1). The ministry of miracles which Christ performed was also according to the prophet Isaiah (Matt. 8:16-18; cf. Isa. 53:4). His ministry to the Gentiles (Matt. 12:15-21; cf. Isa. 42:lf.), His arrest (Matt. 26:47-56) and death on the cross (Matt. 27:35) were all particulars which were revealed by God in Scripture many years before they even came to pass.

The significant fact about this array of Scriptural testimony is that Christ Himself recognized the fact that Scripture made known the purpose of God for Him. He lived and died in the prescribed will of God recorded in Scripture. The repeated phrase "that it might be fulfilled" in many of the above passages is evidence of this fact.

To reveal the person of Christ

One could wish that the interpretation and exposition which Christ gave to the two on the road to Emmaus had been recorded. Luke records that beginning with Moses and through all the prophets on that memorable day He interpreted to them "in all the Scriptures the things concerning himself" (Luke 24:27). In the same context the words of Christ make it clear that the Law, the Prophets and the Psalms or writings all spoke of Him (Luke 24:44).

The Messianic character of the Old Testament was a cherished hope of the Jews. Speaking of their common hope and relation to the heathen world Edersheim says: "That hope pointed them all, wherever scattered, back to Palestine. To them the coming of the Messiah undoubtedly implied the restoration of Israel's kingdom, and, as a first part in it, the return of 'the dispersed.' . . . Hopes and expectations such as these are expressed not only in Talmudic writings. We find them throughout that very interesting Apocalyptic class of literature, the Pseudepigrapha. . . . Fuller details of that happy event are furnished by the Jewish Sibyl. In her utterances these three events are connected together: the coming of the Messiah, the rebuilding of the temple, and the restoration of the dispersed, when all nations would bring their wealth to the House of God."[11]

Thus it can be seen that Biblical as well as extra-Biblical literature substantiates the fact that the Jews were aware of the Messianic content of the Old Testament and strongly supported it.

Christ recognized the Scriptures as the revelation of God concerning His person. Two verses will suffice to establish this proposition.

The Lord cites three witnesses in defense of His deity in John 5. These witnesses in order are His own divine works (v. 36), the witness of the Father (vv. 37, 38), and finally the witness of the Scriptures (v. 39). Our present concern is with the witness of the Scriptures to Christ. To the unbelieving Jews He said, "Ye search the scriptures, because ye think that in them ye have eternal life; and these are they which bear witness of me" (John 5:39).

Christ's teaching is clearly set forth by His candid statement that the Scriptures "bear witness" of Him. The Jewish

---

[11] Alfred Edersheim, *The Life and Times of Jesus the Messiah* (London: Longmans, Green and Co., 1912), pp. 78-79.

Scriptures witnessed of one whom the Jews would not receive. They refused Him and the life which He offered.

Almost in the same breath Christ claimed a smaller portion of the Scriptures as that which revealed His person. He said, "For if ye believed Moses, ye would believe me; for he wrote of me" (John 5:46). He had just established the fact that the Scriptures as a whole witnessed of Him; now He points to the very part of that Scripture (the law) to which they adhered most tenaciously and claims to be the subject of that revelation.

In these words of Christ He acknowledges the purpose of the revelation of God to reveal His own person. The ultimate reason for the Jews' rejection of Him was because they would not believe the Word of God which was given to reveal Him. It is ever the case. Men reject Him because they reject His Word.

Conclusion

Evidence has been presented to show that Christ viewed the Scripture as the revelation of God to man. The means by which the revelation came to be known included Christ as the apex, men through whom God spoke and the words of God given to men. For Christ this revelation was final. It was not yet completed when He spoke though what was completed was truth which was sufficient and binding. The Saviour's testimony was that whatever is found in Scripture is the word of God.

The testimony of Christ to the divine origin of the entire Old Testament Scripture is the united testimony of the writers of both the Old and New Testaments. Citation of all the references is not necessary here. A few of them may be cited, however, to illustrate the point. Such expressions as "Jehovah spake unto" and equivalent terms appear hundreds of times (e.g., see 1 Kings 8:35; 2 Chron. 35:6). The prophets claim divine source for their prophecies (Isa. 1:2; Jer. 1:6-9; Ezek. 1:3; Hos. 1:1; etc.). The New Testament writers bear the same testimony to the divine origin of their own writings and the writings of others (Acts 3:25; 2 Cor. 6:16; Jas. 2:11; 2 Pet. 1:21; 2 Tim. 3:16).

CHAPTER III

THE INSPIRATION OF SCRIPTURE IN THE SAVIOUR'S TEACHING

The inspiration of Scripture is a subject of utmost importance. Every believer ought to know what he believes about this subject and why he believes it. We have seen that Christ believed and taught the divine origin of the Scriptures. The matter now before us is how He viewed this recorded revelation of God. The men who wrote the revelation of God were sinners and Christ made no attempt to gloss over their failures. Nevertheless, Christ emphatically taught the inspiration of what these men wrote. He did not teach the inspiration of the men but He did teach the inspiration of their writings.

DEFINITION OF INSPIRATION

In order to understand the use of the term *inspiration* in the following pages, a formal definition is necessary. Gaussen's classic definition has been acceptable to the orthodox: ". . . . that inexplicable power which the Divine Spirit put forth of old on the authors of holy Scripture, in order to their guidance even in the employment of the words they used, and to preserve them alike from all error and from all omission."[1]

There are several important elements in a true definition of inspiration and all of them are present in Christ's teaching though He never formally gave a definition. Before stating these crucial elements a proper understanding of the word "inspiration" is essential.

---

[1] L. Gaussen, *The Plenary Inspiration of the Holy Scriptures* (Chicago: The Bible Institute Colportage Association, n.d.), p. 34.

The Greek word θεόπνευστος from which the word inspiration comes occurs but once in the New Testament (2 Tim. 3:16). Commenting on its occurrence in this passage Warfield states: "The Greek term has, however, nothing to say of **in**spirating or of **in**spiration: it speaks only of a 'spiring' or 'spiration.' What it says of Scripture is, not that it is 'breathed into by God' or is the product of the Divine 'inbreathing' into its human authors, but that it is breathed out by God, 'God breathed,' the product of the creative breath of God."[2]

Any definition of inspiration which is true to the Biblical concept must include: (1) the divine guidance (2) of the human writers (3) in the choice of words (4) in the original autographs thus keeping them from all error and omission.

Relation of Revelation to Inspiration

Revelation concerns what God has made known; it relates to the unveiling of facts concerning Himself and His will. Inspiration concerns the end product of revelation—the record. It is related to the recording of the revelation which has been made known. The written record in a genuine sense, then, becomes **the** revelation of God to men. Edward J. Young ably distinguishes between the two: "We must therefore make a distinction between revelation and inspiration. It is true that the two are very closely related, and it is true that in the broad sense inspiration is a form or mode of revelation. At the same time, it is well to keep in mind the fundamental distinction that, whereas revelation is essentially the communication of knowledge of information, inspiration is designed to secure infallibility in teaching."[3]

Much of the evidence which has been presented to show that Scripture originated with God might be used to show Christ's view of the inspiration of Scripture. Since Scripture is the recorded revelation of God it will also be accepted as inspired.

---

[2] Benjamin Breckinridge Warfield, *The Inspiration and Authority of the Bible* (Philadelphia: The Presbyterian and Reformed Publishing Company, 1948), p. 133.

[3] Edward J. Young, *Thy Word Is Truth* (Grand Rapids: Wm. B. Eerdmans Publishing Co., 1957), pp. 41-42.

The Saviour believed that the inspiration of Scripture extended not only to the entire record in a general way but also to the most minute details recorded therein.

The Extent of Inspiration

The most casual reading of the Gospels brings one to the fact that Christ accepted and taught a high view of the Scriptures. His very use of them and His firm conviction that behind the human writers God was the ultimate author reveals His estimate of the Scriptures. Though some question His knowledge, and some even His integrity, it is a generally accepted fact that He held high esteem for the Scriptures.

It will be demonstrated here, however, that Christ held more than a general view of the inspiration of Scripture. He taught the full and complete inspiration of the Old Testament in every word and detail and made provision for the same inspiration of the New Testament by His promise of the enabling work of the Holy Spirit.

Inspiration of the Old Testament

Since none of the New Testament was written when Christ was here all of His references to a completed body of writings referred to the Old Testament. It will be seen, however, that He did make clear provision in His teaching for the inspiration of the New Testament writings. No one ever asked Christ if the Scriptures were inspired; that was an accepted fact. Marcus Dods acknowledged this fact. "The OT was accepted as inspired both by the NT writers and by all their Jewish contemporaries. . . . Of this there is abundant evidence. . . . No belief of later Judaism was more universal or constant than this acceptance of the OT Scripture as inspired."[4]

Christ taught the inspiration of the whole Old Testament. Obviously, if it can be proven that He taught the inspiration of individual parts, words and letters, it necessarily follows that He taught the inspiration of the whole. The words of His teaching used to prove the one fact also prove the other. In order to show the extent of His teaching we will begin with

---

[4] Marcus Dods, "Inspiration," *A Dictionary of Christ and the Gospels*, ed. James Hastings, (1907), I 831-32.

His teaching of the whole and proceed to His teaching of the inspiration of the individual parts, words and letters.

Inspiration of the whole: It is obvious from a careful study of the Gospels that Christ viewed the body of writings known as the Old Testament as an organic whole. The Old Testament in His teaching not only constituted a harmonious whole but it also constituted an inspired whole.

To begin, it may be noticed that the plenary inspiration of the entire Old Testament was affirmed by Christ when He said: "Think not that I came to destroy the law, or the prophets: I came not to destroy, but to fulfil. For verily I say unto you, Till heaven and earth pass away, one jot or one tittle shall in no wise pass away from the law, till all things be accomplished" (Matt. 5:17-18). Without doubt, the last part of this quotation grants inspiration to the most minute part of Scripture and it thus also emphatically gives Christ's view of the inspiration of the whole. The Saviour could not have employed stronger words to declare His view because the law and the prophets meant the entire Old Testament Scriptures. " 'The law and the prophets' is a standard title for the Old Testament. This Word stood as God's authoritative revelation from Malachi onward for 430 years until God sent John."[5] Christ's reference to the law does not only mean the ordinances of Judaism because nothing of those ordinances would be known apart from the record in Scripture. Thus, the reference must apply to the Scriptures and to the dispensation of Judaism.

That Christ accepted the inspiration of the whole Old Testament is proven also by His sweeping reference to the threefold division as it existed in His day. He declared that all things must be fulfilled which were written of Him, ". . . in the law of Moses, and the prophets, and the psalms, concerning me" (Luke 24:44). Having said this He opened their minds to the understanding of the Scriptures. Harris concurs on the reference in Matthew 5:17, 18 and Luke 24:44 as both referring to the entire Old Testament. In explanation of Matthew 5:17, 18 he states: ". . . Christ is here referring to a book. The characteristic name for this book in the New Testament is the usual Jewish phrase 'the Law and the Prophets.' This

---

[5] R. C. H. Lenski, *The Interpretation of St. Luke's Gospel* (Columbus: The Wartburg Press, 1946), pp. 839-40.

title or a similar one like 'Moses and the Prophets' is used a dozen times in the New Testament. Once the sacred volume is called 'the law of Moses . . . the prophets, and the psalms' (Luke 24:44). At other times the entire Old Testament is referred to simple as 'the law.' For instance, Jesus quotes a verse outside of the Pentateuch as the 'law' (John 10:30)."[6]

Christ's repeated question, "Have ye not read?" is equivalent to "Do you not know that God has said?" (cf. Matt. 12:3; 19:4; 21:16; 22:31; Mark 2:25; 12:10, 26; Luke 6:3). The very same meaning is to be understood by γέγραπται, "it stands written" (Matt. 11:10; 21:13; 26:24, 31; Mark 9:12, 13; 11:17; 14:21, 27; Luke 7:27; 19:46). Jesus' use of such phrases as these applied equal inspiration to all parts of Scripture—history, laws, psalms and prophecies.

That Christ regarded the entire body of Scripture as a unit, inspired and thus to be fulfilled *in toto,* is seen from His statement in Matthew 26:54. Speaking of His arrest He said, "How then should the scriptures be fulfilled, that thus it must be?" Notice it is the plural Scriptures thus indicating the existence of many writings which possessed the quality of Scripture.

Inspiration of the parts: Christ's references to the Law, Prophets, Psalms or writings section of the Old Testament not only reveal His attitude toward the entire body of Scripture to which these designations referred but also reveal His confidence in the inspiration of each of the parts. For Him the Law was inspired, the Prophets were inspired and the Psalms or writings were inspired. He referred in a comprehensive way to the laws of the Pentateuch as "the commandments of God" as opposed to "the traditions of men" (Mark 7:8, 9). The "it is written" of Matthew 4:4, 7, 10, already referred to, certainly places Christ's unshakable confidence in the portions of Deuteronomy He quotes.

Every reference of Christ to the Scripture as that which must be fulfilled is evidence of the fact that He believed in the complete inspiration of the particular part referred to. He fulfilled the Messianic office that the Scripture might be fulfilled. His preaching was in fulfillment of Scripture (Luke 4:18ff.; cf. Isa. 61:1ff.). He healed in fulfillment of Scripture

---

[6] R. Laird Harris, *Inspiration and Canonicity of the Bible* (Grand Rapids: Zondervan Publishing House, 1957), p. 46.

(Matt. 8:16f.; cf. LXX version of Isa. 53:4). As was true of His entire life and ministry, He went to death in fulfillment of Scripture (Mark 8:31; cf. 9:31; 10:33f.; Matt. 26:24; Luke 22:37, RSV quoting Isa. 53:12).[7]

Inspiration of the words: Pursuing the present line of argument it may be said that Christ not only accepted the whole Old Testament as that which was breathed out by God, not only the individual parts and sections, but He insisted on the inspiration of the very words of Scripture. Nothing in the teaching of Christ indicates that He believed or taught merely concept or thought inspiration. Frequently the weight of His entire argument rested upon one or two words which He quoted from the Old Testament. If that word or those words did not have the authority which He claimed for them His arguments would have been fruitless and would certainly have been recognized as such by His critics who knew the Scriptures so well.

There are three central passages in which Christ emphasized the inspiration and authority of the words of Scripture. In each of these His entire argument is valid only if the words in question were inspired. There are many other references besides these three which teach His high regard and belief in the inspiration of words but these three are crucial. Each of these instances is the result of Christ's dealing with His enemies. This fact is significant, for it emphasizes His own implicit trust in the very Scriptures with which they were seeking to accuse Him. Their fault did not lie in their Scriptures but in their added traditions and false interpretations.

The astonishing answer which Christ gave to the extended and involved question of the Sadducees regarding the resurrection stands or falls on the inspiration of one word and the tense of that word (Matt. 22:23-33). Jesus said, "I am the God of Abraham, and the God of Isaac, and the God of Jacob. God is not the God of the dead, but of the living" (Matt. 22:32). Thus by one verb, translated "I am" in the present tense instead of the past tense "I was," the Saviour proves to the Sadducees the doctrine of the resurrection. Our Lord quoted here from Exodus 3:6 where God said to Moses, four hundred years after Abraham had died, that He was at that time Abraham's God.

---

[7] J. I. Packer, "*Fundamentalism and the Word of God* (Grand Rapids: Wm. B. Eerdmans Publishing Co., 1960), pp. 57-58.

After listening to their involved argument Christ responded by saying: "Ye do err, not knowing the scriptures, nor the power of God" (Matt. 22:29). They were ignorant on two counts. Ignorance of the Scriptures produced ignorance of the power of God, for therein the power of God is revealed. The obvious implication of Christ is that had they known the Scriptures they would have been kept from error. Certainly, that which would have kept them from error must itself be true. M'Intosh summarizes well the importance of the inspiration of the words which Christ quoted to the Sadducees: "Here, too, he founds the truth of the resurrection of the dead on a particular form of the name of God, ay, on the present instead of the past tense of the verb. Have ye not read that which was spoken unto you by God, saying, I *am* the God of Abraham (ἐγὼ εἰμὶ ὁ Θεός Αβραάμ). . . . A great and unexpected truth is here brought out of the special form of expression used, in which the slightest variation would have destroyed the basis of Christ's argument. . . . There is here the proof of supernatural inspiration in the words he wrote; and there is no reasonable explanation of our Lord's founding such a great truth except upon what was the infallible Word of God."[8]

---

[8] Hugh M'Intosh, *Is Christ Infallible and the Bible True?* (Edinburgh: T. & T. Clark, 1901), p. 191.

The above conclusion drawn from this passage has been contested on two grounds. Some acknowledge Christ's emphasis on the present tense but since in the Hebrew the verb is not expressed at all Christ is accused of a false emphasis. Others do not believe Christ's argument is derived from it and therefore the words mean no more than that Jehovah was the God whom Abraham, Isaac and Jacob worshiped.

Johnson argues, against Toy and those who hold such a light view of Christ's quotation, that the absence of the verb in the original in no way weakens Christ's argument. He lists four reasons in defense of His view.

First, Mark's account of the quotation has no verb and thus the argument does not depend upon the presence of the verb in the sentence. *Second,* the Jews to whom the argument was addressed recognized their defeat and it would be absurd to suppose the argument would have produced such an effect if it was falsely based upon the tense of an absent verb. *Third,* it is a law of all languages that words which are omitted but understood are to be considered as expressed. Johnson rightly argues that to make a point of the absence of the verb in the original is to commit the fault with which Christ is charged. *Fourth,* even if it be granted that Christ was merely declaring God to be the one whom the patriarchs worshiped, the inference which He draws from

The second central passage in which Christ teaches the inspiration of the words of Scripture is found in the same chapter (Matt. 22:43-45). It has been shown that this statement and quotation by Christ teaches His belief in the divine origin of Scripture. What David wrote in Psalm 110 he wrote "in the Spirit." The passage teaches more than a general derivation of the Scriptures from God, however. It also teaches the inspiration of even the words of that divine proclamation. His whole argument rests on the second use of the word "Lord" in Psalm 110. "He saith unto them, How then doth David in the Spirit call him Lord, saying, The Lord said unto my Lord, Sit thou on my right hand, Till I put thine enemies underneath thy feet?" (Matt. 22:43-44).

This answer, which stifled any more questions on the part of the Pharisees, shows Christ's use of the Scriptures as the inspired words of God. The answer to the Sadducees concerned the resurrection; this argument concerns His deity and to defend it He alludes to the second use of the word "Lord" in Psalm 110. Actually, Christ is here sustaining His view of the doctrine of the deity of the Messiah on a single word. The amazing thing is that the word involved comes from a Psalm where it could be argued that the Psalmist might have employed a construction without any intention of being so literally interpreted. Yet Christ so minutely interprets the letter of Scripture as to build a whole doctrine upon it because that one word carried the authority of the God who gave it.

The third central passage to be cited in favor of Christ's teaching of the inspiration of words is John 10:33-36. The primary teaching of this passage concerns Christ's view of the authority of Scripture and will be dealt with subsequently. Here it is employed for the purpose of Christ's emphasis on the inspiration of words of Scripture. Both facts are clearly taught in this crucial passage.

The statement of Christ arose as He vindicated Himself from the charge of blasphemy made by the Jews. Again, as in the last passage, Christ is defending and asserting His

---

the declaration stands as necessary and natural. The fact that God so revealed Himself proves the resurrection (Franklin Johnson, *The Quotations of the New Testament from the Old Considered in the Light of General Literature* (Philadelphia: American Baptist Publication Society, 1896), p. 337.

deity. The quotation which He makes from Psalm 82:6, "I said ye are gods," is founded entirely for its validity upon the single word "gods." More than that, the very plural number of the word is essential to His argument.

Christ argues from the infallibility of the word "gods" to the infallibility of the phrase in which it occurs, "I said ye are gods," to the infallibility of the record in which that phrase occurs. That record He ascribes as law though it appears in the Psalms and in a particular Psalm which from every human viewpoint might be considered as rather incidental.

The importance of the inspiration of words as opposed to mere concept or thought inspiration is stated cogently by Miller: "It is sheer nonsense to talk about inspired thoughts apart from inspired words. Dean Burgon, one of England's greatest scholars, said, 'You cannot dissect inspiration into substance and form. As for thoughts being inspired apart from words which give them expression, you might as well talk of a tune without notes or a sum without figures. No such dream can abide the daylight for a moment. It is as illogical as it is worthless, and cannot be too sternly put down.' "[9]

Inspiration of the letters: Our argument thus far has proceeded from the whole to the individual parts. It has been demonstrated that Christ accepted and taught the inspiration of the whole Old Testament, its individual parts and the very words. It will now be shown that He went one step further by teaching the inspiration of the letters and smallest details of the words.

Evidence for this fact appears clearly in two carefully worded statements of the Lord. Just prior to His Sermon on the Mount He said: "For verily I say unto you, Till heaven and earth pass away, one jot or one tittle shall in no wise pass away from the law, till all things be accomplished" (Matt. 5:18). Again, Christ's answer to the scoffing Pharisees gives the same truth: "But it is easier for heaven and earth to pass away, than for one tittle of the law to fall" (Luke 16:17).

The determinative words in these passages are "jot" and "tittle." The "jot" is most likely a reference to the ninth letter of the Greek alphabet (ι) which is the nearest Greek equiva-

---

[9] H. S. Miller, *General Biblical Introduction* (Houghton, New York: The Word-Bearer Press, 1944), p. 25.

lent for the Hebrew yōdh (י) which is the smallest letter of the Hebrew alphabet. The expression refers to the most minute trifles of Scripture.

The tittle is not as easily identified. Harris states the two most common interpretations: "Most take it to refer to the small parts of Hebrew letters which distinguish one from the other, like our dot over the i and cross of the t. Others think it may refer to the Hebrew letter Waw, which often served only to distinguish a long from a short vowel."[10]

The word "tittle" as used by our Lord means the little lines or projections which differentiate certain Hebrew letters which in other respects are similar. To alter one small point or "tittle" might change the meaning of the word or at least change the sense of it. It is thus abundantly clear from Christ's teaching that the minutest part of the law as originally written must be accomplished. He taught the inspiration of the very letters.

Also, on the basis of His teaching in Matthew 22:32 and John 10:34 it may even be said that He accepted the inspiration of the tense and number of the grammatical constructions.

Certainly, our Lord did not intend to teach in these passages that the actual letters and markings which appeared on the writing materials of original documents would endure forever. If that had been His intention His enemies would have found it very easy to disprove Him because not only were the original documents not available when He spoke but many copies were also already extant. No, to believe that by these statements Christ taught the verbal inspiration of the Old Testament Scripture is not hindered by the fact that we do not possess the original documents on which those first "jots" and "tittles" appeared. What then did the Saviour mean by these bold assertions? In answer to that question one thing is abundantly clear. He was speaking of law or Scripture which was *written* and not merely the concept or truth of Scripture. Critics have always attempted to tone down the Saviour's teaching here by either denying that these words were really the Lord's, or by reversing His emphasis altogether and saying He intended to stress the spirit of the law instead of the letter,[11] or by making these words refer

---

[10] Harris, *op. cit.*, pp. 46-47.

[11] Dewey M. Beegle, *The Inspiration of Scripture* (Philadelphia: The Westminster Press, 1963), pp. 73-75.

to the unwritten principle of the law or still further by naively acknowledging that these and other words simply teach the Saviour's high regard for the Old Testament but not His belief in verbal inspiration.[12] The answer which Warfield gave long ago to one such critic, Richard Rothe, still stands in relation to the "jot" and "tittle" references. ". . . it is the law itself *as written* that the Lord has in mind, in which form alone, moreover, do 'yodhs and horns' belong to it. . . ."[13]

If the Saviour was teaching anything at all by these words, "jot" and "tittle," and the fact of their durability He was teaching that the most minute portions and trifles of the Old Testament as originally written, the very markings which gave meanings to words of Scripture, would not fail of fulfillment because they came from God and were thus absolutely inerrant. This high view of Scripture is the Bible's testimony to itself time and time again (e.g., I Cor. 2:13; Gal. 3:16).

Summarily, then, the evidence from Christ's teaching for the inspiration of the Old Testament is complete. He not only accepted the whole Old Testament as the inspired Word of God but the individual parts and words were viewed by Him as possessing the very accuracy and authority of the God who gave them.

The fact of the Saviour's belief in the verbal plenary inspiration of Scripture is acknowledged by many scholars. Gaussen says: ". . . one is compelled to rank him among the most ardent partisans of verbal inspiration, and that we do not think, that had we before us all the writings of divines the most uncompromising in their orthodoxy, we should any where find an example of more profound respect for the letter of Scripture, and for the plentitude of their divine inspiration."[14] Wenham also acknowledges this fact: ". . . that some sort of verbal inspiration is taught by Christ is clear, seeing that it is to the writings rather than to the writers that He ascribes authority. Writings are made up of words, therefore there must be some form of word-inspiration."[15]

---

[12] Daniel B. Stevick, *Beyond Fundamentalism* (Richmond, John Knox Press, 1964), pp. 87-88.

[13] Warfield, *op. cit.*, p. 184.

[14] Gaussen, *op. cit.*, p. 102.

[15] J. W. Wenham, *Our Lord's View of the Old Testament* (London: The Tyndale Press, 1953), p. 25.

The witness of Christ to the inspiration of the Old Testament in its whole and in every part is substantiated by the faith and testimony of the Jews of His day and also by the Christian church.

Those Jews who were contemporary with Christ and with the New Testament writers taught clearly the divine origin and thus inspiration of every word of the Old Testament. The Apocryphal books, which Christ never quoted, bear witness to the canonical books of the Old Testament. The books of the Old Testament were "the holy books of Scripture" (1 Maccabees 12:9). The law was given by God and Moses was God's spokesman and writer (Ecclesiasticus 24:23; 28:7; Wisdom 11:1). Jeremiah spoke "from the mouth of the Lord" (Esdras 1:28).

Philo, the Jewish philosopher, also recognized the complete inspiration of the Old Testament. Shearton writes: "It was affirmed, e.g., by Philo, who set forth an elaborate theory of inspiration, that every portion of every book was written under divine inspiration, and that knowledge of all matters which could not naturally be acquired by the prophets was communicated to them by direct revelation from God."[16]

Josephus, the Jewish historian contemporary with Christ, agrees with the testimony of Philo regarding the inspiration of the Old Testament. He accepted every part as written by a prophet and the prophet's words as God's words. Concerning Moses he writes, ". . . whatsoever he pronounced you would think you heard the voice of God."[17]

With the exception of a few heretics the church held the same high view of the Old Testament as that endorsed by Christ. Expressions such as "the Scripture saith," "it is written," "He [God] saith" and other expressions which attribute to the human writers divine superintendence are found frequently in many of the church fathers.

Inspiration of the New Testament

Every reference which Christ made to the Scriptures in any of the designations which He employed was a reference to the Old Testament. What of the New Testament? Did

[16] J. P. Shearton, "The Process of Inspiration," *The Bible Student and Teacher*, I (January, 1904), 16.

[17] Josephus, *Antiquities of the Jews*, iv, 49.

Christ teach anything which would indicate His view of the writings which were to compose the New Testament?

The position of Christ: Christ stands between the Old and New Testaments. He placed His divine approval upon every jot and tittle of the Old Testament. Likewise, in anticipation He guaranteed the inspiration of the New Testament by His promise of the Holy Spirit. He looked back upon that which was already written as the inspired Word of God. He looked ahead and assured the writers of the New Testament of the same divine superintendence of the Holy Spirit as had guided the Old Testament writers, thus granting inspiration to their written product. His position then was unique in that He pronounced upon the inspiration of the Old and promised inspiration for the New. Bruce shows clearly Christ's relation to the Old and New Testaments: "For it was the Old Testament Scriptures that constituted Christ's Bible. . . . Does this mean we receive the New Testament on lower authority than the Old? Not really; it only means that the impartation of Christ's authority to the New is less immediately apparent. But when we look into the matter we find that He who accredited the Old Testament retrospectively accredited the New Testament prospectively."[18]

The provision of Christ: This prospective accreditation appears in several places and involves several things. First of all, it must be understood that Christ made provision for the writing of the New Testament. He made it clear that God's act of revealing truth was not finished. He said, "I have yet many things to say unto you but ye cannot bear them now" (John 16:12). The Holy Spirit was to come and complete the revelation. Christ recognized that the canon of Scripture was not closed at the time of His death. The promise of guidance into further truth is evidence of that fact (John 15:26, 27; 16:13). Thus through His teaching He allowed for the New Testament and gave it His pre-authentication.

Christ not only occupied a unique position between the Old and New Testaments and made provision for the writing of the New Testament but He also promised divine guidance to the disciples by the ministry of the Holy Spirit.

---

[18] F. F. Bruce, *The Books and the Parchments* (London: Pickering & Inglis Ltd., 1950), p. 103.

The promise of Christ in inspiration: On five different occasions Jesus promised to His apostles the aid of the Holy Spirit in their utterances. These five instances are not all of equal pertinence; yet they all clearly set forth the promises of divine aid to the writers of the New Testament.

C. I. Scofield has summarized Christ's pre-authentication of the New Testament under four headings: "(1) He expressly declared that He would leave 'many things' unrevealed (v.12). (2) He promised that this revelation should be completed ('all things') after the Spirit should come, and that such additional revelation should include new prophecies (v. 13). (3) He chose certain persons to receive such additional revelations, and to be His witnesses to them (Mt. 28:19; John 15:27; 16:13; Acts 1:8; 9:15-17). (4) He gave to their words when speaking for Him in the Spirit precisely the same authority as His own (Mt. 10:14, 15; Lk. 10:16; John 13:20, 17:20; see e.g., 1 Cor. 14:37, and 'Inspiration,' Ex. 4:15; Rev. 22:19)."[19]

Christ's promise of the ministry of the Holy Spirit in the work of New Testament inspiration is concisely stated in John 14:26, "But the Comforter, even the Holy Spirit, whom the Father will send in my name, he shall teach you all things, and bring to your remembrance all that I said unto you." Two central truths are taught in this passage. Christ said the Spirit would teach them all things and bring all things which Christ said to their remembrance. The parallel passage in John 15:26, 27 shows that the Holy Spirit would bear witness to Christ. Thus He would teach and bring to mind those things which Christ taught. The entire New Testament is an amplification of that which Christ taught.

The promise of Christ in illumination: In connection with Christ's teaching of the inspiration of the New Testament a word should be said about His promise of the illuminating work of the Holy Spirit for the understanding of Scripture.

The need for such a work was acknowledged often by Christ as He dealt both with His disciples and with the Pharisees and scribes. Christ began the work of illumination after His resurrection with the two on the Emmaus road and

---

[19] C. I. Scofield (ed.), *The Scofield Reference Bible* (New York: Oxford University Press, 1909), p. 1138.

to those gathered in the upper room. "Then opened he their mind, that they might understand the scriptures" (Luke 22:44). The work which Christ began to do He promised would be continued by the Holy Spirit (John 16:13). Therefore, the writers of the New Testament were not left to their own decisions as to what to write and neither are the readers left unaided to understand what is written. The same Spirit who inspired the record is the one who illuminates the mind to understand it.

The proof of Christ's promises: The proof for the teaching and guiding work of the Holy Spirit as promised by Christ is given ample testimony by the New Testament writers themselves (1 Cor. 2:9-12; 7:24; 2 Peter 3:1-2; Rev. 1:1-2). Not only did the writers of the New Testament claim the authority of God for their own writings but they also claimed that authority for the writings of others (1 Tim. 5:18; 2 Pet. 3:16). Thus the work of the Holy Spirit promised by Christ was acknowledged by those on whom He performed His ministry.

There is an indirect line of proof for Christ's teaching of the inspiration of the New Testament to be found in the word *Scriptures.* As has been indicated, when Christ used the term it referred only to the Old Testament canon. However, the word *Scripture* came to be used soon after Christ's departure as a designation for the New Testament as well as the Old. The apostles and church fathers made no distinction between the Old and New Testaments in their use of the term *Scripture.*

Paul in writing to Timothy quotes Luke along with Deuteronomy as "scripture" (1 Tim. 5:18). Peter designates the writings of Paul "scripture" (2 Pet. 3:16). Thus even before the close of the canon they were placing one another's writings in the class of Old Testament Scripture. And of course later, the entire New Testament was called "Scripture."

The early Christians entertained the same profound respect for the Old Testament as the Jews did but they also received by universal consent the Scriptures of the New Testament. Both Testaments were regarded by them as the Oracles of God. The church fathers set forth the same testimony. The united testimony of such fathers as Clement of Rome, Justin Martyr, Irenaeus, Theophilus, Clement of Alexandria and Origen is that the New Testament is divine Scripture as is also the Old Testament.

Christ's teaching of the inspiration of the New Testament then, may be established from several considerations. His unique position between the Testaments as the one who unequivocally placed His approval, in agreement with the Jews of His day, upon the inspiration of the Old Testament, and His provision that further revelation would be given by the Holy Spirit argues for the proposition. Also, His explicit promises of the Spirit's guidance in writing and understanding the future revelation can only be understood as His stamp of approval upon all that the apostles would write while under the Spirit's control. Finally, it may also be adduced, in addition to the above evidence, that since the entire New Testament came to be known as Scripture along with the Old Testament, Christ's repeated references to Scripture speak prophetically of the New Testament, thus ascribing to it the same inspiration as the Old Testament possessed.

The Results of Inspiration

Such a high and exalted view of Scripture carries with it certain concomitant truths. No one could believe the Scriptures originated with God as the Saviour did and believe they are in error, for God cannot lie. If the words of Scripture in the original autographs are the very words of God, breathed out by Him in every detail, as Christ taught, they must of necessity be inerrant, infalliable and therefore authoritative.

The results to be listed here were not stated by Christ in these terms. With the exception of the word *authority* these terms are not Biblical but theological and were not used in His day. Nevertheless, the meaning and significance of these words were clearly taught by Christ in His references to the Scriptures. His acceptance and teaching of the inspiration of Scripture as outlined above lead to the following resultant truths.

Inerrancy and infallibility

Definitions: These words are often used today without proper definition. After defining them it will be shown that Christ taught what is meant by these words with regard to the Scriptures. Inerrancy and infallibility are almost synonymous terms. When used in reference to Scripture we mean that Scripture is totally free from error or mistake and that it therefore possesses indefectible authority.

Positive considerations: Because of the similarity in the meanings of these terms they will be considered synonymous in the present discussion. That this inerrancy and infallibility extends to the words of Scripture has been presented above as the teaching of Christ. One can argue either from His acceptance of the whole Old Testament to the parts and words or from the words and parts to the whole. To say He taught one is to say He taught the other. Though several passages might be adduced in support of this proposition, Matthew 5:17-19 and Luke 16:17 are the most central. If the Scriptures must be fulfilled even to the jot, the smallest Hebrew letter, and the tittle, the distinguishing stroke on certain Hebrew letters, they obviously must be as inerrant and infallible as the God who gave them.

The cumulative evidence presented above for word and letter inspiration logically leads to verbal inerrancy and infallibility. Christ did not teach mere thought or concept inpiration. His sole emphasis was upon the words, the writing of Scripture. "Scripture means writing (that which is written) and writing is composed of words and letters."[20]

To construe Christ's teaching of Scripture as anything less than complete inerrancy and absolute infallibility is to accuse either Him, the Gospel writers, or both, of the crassest sort of ignorance and hypocrisy. He used the Scriptures for Himself and for others with complete reliance upon their absolute accuracy. This inerrancy He not only applied to matters of ethics and morals but to matters of history and geography as well. Too, His teaching of inerrancy and infallibility applies both to revelational and non-revelational matters, to that which the writer only knew through special divine revelation and to that which was already known as matters of history.

It logically follows that if the ultimate source of Scripture is God, which fact Christ emphatically taught, the record is without error and is trustworthy. Long ago, Warfield wrote of the relation of these two facts. "Revelation is but half revelation unless it be infallibly communicated; it is but half communicated unless it be infallibly recorded."[21]

---

[20] Edward J. Young, *Thy Word Is Truth* (Grand Rapids: Wm. B. Eerdmans Publishing Co., 1957), p. 44.

[21] Benjamin Breckinridge Warfield, *Revelation and Inspiration* (New York: Oxford University Press, 1927), p. 424.

Argument from silence: The above evidence is enhanced by the amazing fact that Christ nowhere even so much as alludes to an error in Scripture. Those who would object to this argument most vigorously are usually those who use it most frequently to suit their own purpose. Destructive critics of Scripture use this argument to deny the Mosaic authorship of the Pentateuch and to defend the deutero-authorship of Isaiah. Actually, this is a very strong argument in favor of Christ's teaching of inerrancy. This is so because He never hesitated to speak out against other errors, especially those related to the Scriptures. It is an obvious and recurring fact that Christ sternly rebuked the Jews for their traditions and additions to the Scriptures. Yet He never uttered a word to indicate that He supposed their Scriptures were not true. We must account for this silence. There is a threefold alternative: *first,* there are no errors in Scripture, *second,* Scripture contains errors but the Saviour did not know it, *third,* He knew about the errors but chose not to tell them. If Christ was what He claimed to be and what the New Testament writers made Him out to be, only the first alternative can be accepted.

Authenticity and Genuineness

It is a foregone conclusion that if Scripture is God-breathed and thus inerrant and infallible it is also authentic and genuine.

To say the Bible is authentic is to say it possesses authority since it is the production of the professed human authors. As has already been pointed out, Christ named only four human writers of Scripture and associated them with their writings. It is indeed significant that the authors He did name are the very ones frequently called in question today. Though He named only four human authors His entire use of Scripture and positive teaching of its inspiration unquestionably argues for His belief in the Scriptures as the record of actual facts. Furthermore His confidence in God as the divine author lends conclusive proof to the point in question.

While authenticity refers to authorship, genuineness refers to truth. Out of the mass of testimony to the integrity of the Word, Christ's use of Scripture with Satan during His temptation is probably the clearest. Christ's use of the perfect tense ("it stands written") three times with three different passages from Deuteronomy is strong defense for His acceptance, in the presence of the Arch-enemy of God, of the unchanged and unchangeable Word of God. The Saviour's use of this phrase with Scripture connotes the idea that the issue in question was thus settled because God had spoken.

Authority and Credibility

Since an entire chapter will be devoted to Christ's teaching on the authority of Scripture the subject need not be discussed at length here. It is only a natural and necessary conclusion that if the Scriptures are all that the Lord said they were, they are authoritative in everything upon which they pronounce. Christ so used the Word in every circumstance of life.

That the Scriptures are credible means they possess the right to be believed and received because of their absolute truthfulness. This point has already been established and need not be labored here. The evident fact that Christ so emphasized the need of the Scriptures for His friends and foes is sufficient testimony to His faith in their credibility.

CONCLUSION

This chapter has been occupied with Christ's teaching of the inspiration of Scripture. His testimony bears witness to the inspiration of the Old Testament in its entirety and in all its individual parts. Also, it has been demonstrated that Christ made provision for the writing of the New Testament and promised the gift of the Holy Spirit as a pledge of truth and a guard against error to the writers in its production. The significance of His view of the God-breathed Scriptures results in His acceptance of their total inerrancy, absolute infallibility, authenticity, genuineness, authority and credibility.

A fitting conclusion to the chapter has been stated by Gaussen in his discussion of John 10:35: "Is it possible to admit that the Being who makes such a use of the Scriptures Does Not Believe in Their Plenary Verbal Inspiration? And if he could have imagined that the words of the Bible were left to the free choice and pious fancies of the sacred writers, would he ever have dreamed of founding such arguments on such a word? The Lord Jesus, our Saviour and our Judge, believed then in the most complete inspiration of the Scriptures; and for him the first rule of all hermeneutics, and the commencement of all exegesis, was this simple maxim applied to the most minute expressions of the written word, 'And The Scripture Cannot Be Broken.' "[22]

[22] Gaussen, *op. cit.*, p. 105.

Chapter IV

THE AUTHORITY OF SCRIPTURE IN THE SAVIOUR'S TEACHING

The Saviour's teaching regarding the source of Scripture and the inspiration of Scripture is clear and abundant. The question now before us is a question of authority. What authority did Christ place upon this divinely-originated and inspired Scripture which He used so freely and extensively. Before that question can be answered accurately we must have the meaning of the word "authority."

Definition and Relationships

By the authority of Scripture, therefore, is meant that it is the ultimate and final mediated standard of truth and criterion for judgment and evaluation. All authority ultimately rests with God but because of His transcendence He has mediated His authority to man in the Scriptures of the Old Testament.

Christ, it has already been seen, taught that Scripture originated with God and was revealed by Him. He also taught that the revelation of God in Scripture was therefore, because of its divine source, the inspired Word of God. It is yet to be demonstrated that the Scripture which was revealed by God and inspired by Him is thereby authoritative and final in all its pronouncements. The authority of Scripture rests firmly upon the authority of God and possesses all the authority which He possesses since it came from Him.

This chapter will be divided into three major divisions. *First,* the authority of Christ as it relates to the authority of Scripture will be considered. While He claimed irrevocable authority for His own words He submitted Himself to the authority of the Old Testament. *Second,* Christ's teaching of the authority of the Old Testament and the relationship of revelation, inspiration, canonicity and historicity to authority will be examined. *Third,* Christ's teaching of the authority of the New Testament will be discussed.

The Authority of Christ

As an alternative to the authority of the Bible there is a popular trend to claim the authority of Christ. Those who hold such a view do not deny that Christ used the Old Testament Scriptures but they claim He stands above them and sometimes improves them. Illustrative of this view is the attitude of Reid with regard to Christ's attitude toward the Scriptures: "From the New Testament it may be gathered that the references which, implicit or explicit, He makes to the Old Testament fall into two classes. There is a class of sayings (or actions) in which He improves upon what is written in the Scriptures He knew, and another where He endorses what is there."[1] For proof that He improved upon the Old Testament recourse is usually made to Christ's statements in the Sermon on the Mount. We shall investigate this claim subsequently.

The testimony of others to Christ's authority

The Gospel writers: Speaking of the purpose of the Gospels Lloyd-Jones observes: "These Gospels were written with a definite and deliberate objective in view. They were not just written as records or as mere collections of facts. No, there is no question at all but that they had a particular point of view to present. They all present the Lord Jesus Christ as the Lord, as this final authority."[2]

Matthew's orderly presentation of Jesus the Son of David and the Son of Abraham as the Messiah of Israel reveals his recognition of the authority of Jesus. The specific application of the Old Testament word "Immanuel" to Christ speaks of His divine authority.

---

[1] J. K. S. Reid, *The Authority of Scripture* (New York: Harper and Brothers, n.d.), pp. 260-61.

[2] D. Martyn Lloyd-Jones, *Authority* (Chicago: Inter-Varsity Press, 1958), p. 16.

Mark presents Christ as the one who has the authority to announce the good tidings of God and the kingdom of God (Mark 1:14-15).

Luke recognized that Christ was "full of the Holy Spirit" (Luke 4:1) and that He worked in the "power of the Spirit" (Luke 4:14). Likewise Luke acknowledged Christ's authority when he said in writing the introduction to the book of Acts: "The former treatise I made, O Theophilus, concerning all that Jesus began both to do and to teach" (Acts 1:1). This reference to the Gospel of Luke demonstrates Luke's acceptance of the authority of Christ as seen in the record of His words and works recorded in the Gospel. Too, Luke's record of the healing ministry of Peter and John and their candid admission of the authority of the name of Jesus argues for Christ's authority (Acts 3:1-16).

John pictures Christ as the Son of God who imparts divine life to those who believe in Him (John 20:31). To do this Christ had to possess authority—divine authority.

Other New Testament writers: Only a few examples from the array of witnesses of the New Testament writers is necessary to substantiate this thesis. Most of these testimonies revolve around the deity and lordship of Christ.

The divine nature of Christ witnessed by the term "Son of God" testifies to His authority. By virtue of the fact that He is the Second Person of the Godhead He possesses absolute authority.

The term ὁ Κύριος ("the Lord") is of great importance since it is applied frequently to Christ in the New Testament. There has been a lot of investigation and debate over the meaning of this term. It must be concluded that the term was used as an address of honor (i.e., when it appeared in the vocative case) as well as a designation of deity.

Christ is sometimes designated as God by the authors of the New Testament. Old Testament texts which originally applied to Jehovah are often applied to Christ (Rom. 10:11; Phil. 2:10; 1 Cor. 1:31; 10:17; 2 Tim. 4:14; Eph. 4:8). Also in Hebrews 1:8, 9 Christ is called "God" twice.

Paul claims to be a servant of Jesus Christ and separated unto the gospel of God. He preached Christ and that message was the gospel of God. Peter denounces any other authority than the authority of Christ and declares that in the message of Christ which he preached there was the power or authority of Christ (2 Pet. 1:16). Again Peter declares that ". . . angels and authorities and powers" were "made subject unto him" (1 Pet. 3:22). To the Colossians Paul said "For in him dwelleth all the fulness of the Godhead bodily" (Col. 2:9). To the Philippians he said Christ possessed a name at which every knee should bow (Phil. 2:9-11). "In 1 Corinthians 2:8 and James 2:1 He is called the 'Lord of Glory,' an expression so often used of God in the Old Testament."[3] The writer of the book of Hebrews ascribes supreme authority to Christ by describing His person and His work (Heb. 1:1-2) as that which climaxes previous revelation.

John the Baptist: Luke records the reaction of some of the multitude to whom John preached by saying, " . . . all men reasoned in their hearts concerning John, whether haply he were the Christ" (Luke 3:15). John turns on them with scorn and his reply vindicates the authority of Christ. John said: " . . . I indeed baptize you with water; but there cometh he that is mightier than I, the latchet of whose shoes I am not worthy to unloose: he shall baptize you in the Holy Spirit and in fire: whose fan is in his hand, thoroughly to cleanse his threshing floor, and to gather the wheat into his garner; but the chaff he will burn up with unquenchable fire" (Luke 3:16).

The prevailing force of John's reply is to the effect that he does not have the Messianic authority which the people desired to ascribe to him but there was one coming who did—namely Christ.

The voice from heaven: There is an important emphasis upon the supreme authority of Christ in the words of the voice from heaven at the baptism and the transfiguration of Christ. As authentication to the authority of Christ at a time when it appeared He was submitting to the authority of John in baptism the voice from heaven said: "This is my beloved Son, in whom I am well pleased" (Matt. 3:17).

Again, at a time when the selected disciples might be tempted to unduly exalt Moses and Elijah the voice proclaims: "This is my beloved Son, in whom I am well pleased; hear ye him" (Matt. 17:5). The conclusion of Geldenhuys on these

[3] F. Norval Geldenhuys, *Supreme Authority* (Grand Rapids: Wm. B. Eerdmans Publishing Company, 1953), p. 34.

two declarations is to the point: "Accordingly by these two announcements, made through the heavenly voice of God the Father at two of the most critical stages in the ministry of our Lord, the Almighty finally and unequivocally proclaimed for all time that Jesus as His beloved Son is indeed clothed with supreme, divine authority. And it is significant that in the announcement at the Transfiguration God, through the voice from heaven, after having said 'This is My beloved Son,' gave the explicit command: 'Hear ye Him!' "[4]

The angelic voice to Mary (Luke 1:33,35) and to the shepherds (Luke 2:10) gives added testimony to the authority of Christ. The angel said He was to be given "the throne of His father David" and was to be the Saviour, "Christ the Lord." Thus those creatures which are dependent upon the Saviour for their existence (Col. 1:16, 17) join chorus with the host of others who declared His impeccable authority.

Mary the mother of Christ: The authority of Christ was declared by His mother at the wedding in Cana of Galilee. The particular area in which He demonstrated His authority was in the realm of nature. His mother's explicit confidence in His authority is seen in her words to the servants who were in an embarrassing position. She said "Whatsoever he saith unto you, do it" (John 2:5). Mary had accepted His authority previously, as early as the temple experience when He was only twelve and now she instructs the servants to do the same.

The testimony of Christ to His own authority

Testimony to the source of His authority: From the beginning of His public ministry to the time of His death and after His resurrection Christ claimed absolute authority both by His words and His works. He not only claimed divine authority, He exercised His authority in all of His ministry. The multitudes acknowledged His unique authority. Matthew records that ". . . the multitudes were astonished at his teaching: for he taught them as one having authority, and not as their scribes" (Matt. 7:28-29). The scribes always appealed to tradition and thus their message was not self-authenticating. They claimed authority but had difficulty substantiating their claims. "With Jesus it was the opposite. He appealed to no tradition, sheltered Himself behind no venerable name, claimed

[4] *Ibid.*, p. 19.

no official status; but those who heard Him could not escape the consciousness that His word was with authority (Luke 4:32). He spoke a final truth, laid down an ultimate law."[5]

The Old Testament prophets, with whom the Jews had been accustomed, never dared to speak in their own name with such authority. They always made it explicitly clear that they spoke with the authority of God. Their words "Thus saith the Lord," occur over and over again in the Old Testament. No wonder the people were amazed and astonished at one who did not appeal to the rabbis or any other external authority but said, "Verily I say unto you" (John 5:25).

The source of such authority is God and since He was God He could thus speak. The Gospel writers make it very clear that Christ's authority was derived from God, His Father. He had been sent by the Father to do the work of the Father and to declare the words of the Father. This commission He fulfilled through the power and authority of the Father (John 17:6-8).

Christ's own testimony was that He came as the fulfiller of the Law and the Prophets (Matt. 5:17). The outworking of His fulfillment of the Old Testament Scriptures, in His ministry, made it clear that His authority exceeded that of the scribes and that the Old Testament Scriptures were anticipatory of Him. His claims and demonstrations of supreme and absolute authority are in complete agreement with the general tenor of the Old Testament. The writers of the Old Testament did not claim authority for themselves. They spoke in the authority of God and looked forward to the Messiah. When Christ came He not only claimed to be the Messiah (John 4:26) but claimed to complete and fulfil that which was spoken of Him in the Old Testament. The Lord accepted this anticipation of Himself and He carefully distinguished in His ministry between His own natural and eternal Sonship and the derived sonship of His followers (Mark 12:1-12; John 20:17).

Upon occasion the chief priests and elders of the people asked Christ the kind and source of His authority. He did not give them a categorical reply but told the parable of the vineyard instead (Matt. 21:23-27, 37; Mark 11:28-33; 12:6;

[5] James Denney, "Authority of Christ," *A Dictionary of Christ and the Gospels*, ed. James Hastings, I (1906), 146.

Luke 20:2, 8, 13). It is clear from His reply to their question that He represents the son referred to in the parable. Those prophets and teachers that were before Him were servants but He is the Son. John records the words of Christ which specifically found His authority in His Sonship. Christ said God gave Him ". . . authority to execute judgment, because he is the Son of man" (John 5:27). Thus Christ traces His authority to His divine Sonship. It may be concluded therefore that the authority of Christ is the authority of God (John 8:23; 12:49; 14:10; 7:17, 18).

There are many examples from the words and works of Christ to set forth His teaching His own authority.

Testimony of His words: Without repeating what has already been said about the Sermon on the Mount it may be noticed that here Christ claimed authority which none else but God could claim. The emphatic and repeated "I" which Christ uses deliberately sets Him forth as the authoritative teacher. Christ had not been to the schools. He was not a Pharisee and yet He does not hesitate to boldly declare, "I say unto you." Since the Sermon dealt primarily with moral issues His words in it become an assertion of His moral authority. The authority which He claimed in the Sermon transcended even the highest known in Israel. Of particular interest in this connection are the Lord's words of conclusion to His Sermon: "Every one therefore that heareth these words of mine and doeth them, shall be likened unto a wise man, who built his house upon the rock" (Matt. 7:24). "There, you see, His whole emphasis is upon 'these sayings of mine.' Here is His claim to final authority. And if it is possible to add to such a statement. He did so when He said, 'Heaven and earth shall pass away, but *my* words shall not pass away.' There is nothing beyond that."[6]

Christ revealed His absolutely supreme authority by the very way in which He spoke. His use of the word "verily" is highly significant. It was customary in Jewish as well as Christian literature outside the Gospels to place the word "verily" at the end of a sentence. In contrast to that method Christ solemnly placed it at the beginning of His declarations. His "verily I say unto you" places Him in a position quite apart from the prophets and the scribes. The prophets intro-

[6] Lloyd-Jones, *op. cit.*, p. 19.

duced their messages with "thus saith the Lord." The scribes claimed tradition as their authority. The Saviour said "I say unto you."

Authority over the church and the kingdom was claimed by Christ. To Peter He said " . . . upon this rock I will build my church; and the gates of Hades shall not prevail against it" (Matt. 16:18). Emphasis is upon the dual facts that He would build the church and that He would guarantee its protection.

Concerning the kingdom of heaven He said only those who know Him could enter (Matt. 7:21f.). Also, He declares His purpose to sit as the King on the throne to judge who is to inherit the kingdom (Matt. 25:3-46). Only one with divine authority could make such stupendous claims.

The authority of Christ over life and salvation is asserted by Him (John 14:6; 17:2). He set Himself up as the only means whereby a man could approach God. There was no selfish motive in the possession of this authority, for Christ prayed that the Father would be glorified through the Son's authority.

As Christ stood before the Sanhedrin in seeming defeat of all He ever claimed, He made the astounding proclamation of His own absolute authority by saying, " . . . Henceforth ye shall see the Son of man sitting on the right hand of Power, and coming on the clouds of heaven" (Matt. 26:64).

After His resurrection Christ reiterated the same claims to authority with equally binding force. To the disciples He said: ". . . All authority hath been given unto me in heaven and earth. Go ye therefore, and make disciples of all the nations, baptizing them in the name of the Father and of the Son and of the Holy Spirit" (Matt. 28:18-19).

A study of the Gospels reveals that Christ claimed absolute authority in every realm. His is authority in the moral realm, over the church, over nature and the evil spirits, and in an all-inclusive way over the entire universe. To Him was given all authority in heaven above and earth beneath. To this stupendous claim of Christ the Apostle Paul agrees when he said God set Him ". . . far above all rule, and authority, and power, and dominion, and every name that is named, not only in this world, but also in that which is to come" (Eph. 1:21).

Testimony of His works: It will only be necessary to mention a few of the works of Christ by which He verified His claims to be authoritative. The Gospels reveal that He not only spoke with authority but that He consistently acted with authority in a unique way.

The call of His disciples is exemplary of His authority. He claimed the men by saying, ". . . Come ye after me, and I will make you fishers of men" (Matt. 4:19). Peter and Andrew obeyed this voice of authority because ". . . they straightway left the nets, and followed him" (Matt. 4:20).

The miracles of Christ are demonstrations of His sovereign power, rule and authority. The exercise of His power over sickness, disease and death, over men, Satan and demons authenticates His authoritative claims.

Christ's ability to raise the dead is certainly indicative of His authority even over death. After raising the dead son of the widow ". . . fear took hold on all: and they glorified God, saying, A great prophet is arisen among us: and, God hath visited his people" (Luke 7:16). Not only did Christ raise others to life and thus demonstrate His power over death but He also arose from the dead Himself thus demonstrating the same in His own life.

Christ as the forgiver of sins provides unmistakable evidence of His authority. He said to the helpless paralytic, ". . . Son, be of good cheer; thy sins are forgiven" (Matt. 9:2). The authority which Christ thus displayed was communicated to His critics, for they said, ". . . This man blasphemeth" (Matt. 9:3). The multitudes also recognized His authority, for ". . . they were afraid, and glorified God, who had given such authority unto men" (Matt. 9:8). Christ proved therefore by healing and forgiving the palsied man that He had the authority to do that which only God could do (Mark 2:10).

Thus it is plain that both in His claims and His deeds Christ testified and bore witness to His divine authority. He spoke with a finality and absoluteness that cannot be gainsaid. He placed His words and the words of the Scriptures on an equal level. It will be remembered that of the Scripture He said, ". . . Till heaven and earth pass away, one jot or one tittle shall in no wise pass away from the law, till all things be accomplished" (Matt. 5:18). Likewise, of His own words He said, "Heaven and earth shall pass away, but my words shall not pass away" (Matt. 24:35).

The submission of His authority to the authority of Scripture

General considerations: It has been demonstrated above that Christ laid claim to His own absolute and unqualified authority. "He appealed to no human authority, but put His teaching forward as divine in origin and therefore eternally valid in its own right. 'My doctrine is not mine, but his that sent me.' "[7] Evidence has been presented to show that He did not hesitate to challenge or condemn on the basis of His own authority. It must be remembered, however, that with all of the emphasis of Christ upon His own authority He never rejected the principle of the equally supreme authority of Scripture. ". . . He never opposed His personal authority to that of the Old Testament. . . . The fact we have to face is that Jesus Christ, the Son of God incarnate, who claimed divine authority for all that He did and taught, both confirmed the absolute authority of the Old Testament for others and submitted to it unreservedly Himself."[8]

It will not be necessary to review here again Christ's use of Scripture and His complete recognition of the revelation and inspiration of Scripture. The arguments presented previously in these pages set forth Christ's acceptance of and dependence upon the authority of Scripture. The issue in His teaching is not over the authority of Scripture versus His own authority but rather the unity of His authority with the authority of Scripture. The authority which He claimed for Himself and the authority which He claimed for the Scriptures are so interwoven that to reject one is to reject both and to receive one is to receive both.

One's view of the Old Testament clearly determines his view of Christ and vice versa. Since Christ never judged Scripture but always obeyed and fulfilled it and endorsed it by word and deed His self-claimed authority must never be set in opposition to the authority of Scripture. Nothing could be more clearly stated than Christ's repeated exhortation to all men to acknowledge and live by the absolute and inviolable authority of Scripture. The authority of Christ would not be known apart from the authoritative record of it in the Scriptures.

---

[7] J. I. Packer, *"Fundamentalism" and the Word of God* (Grand Rapids: Wm. B. Eerdmans Publishing Co., 1960), p. 54.

[8] *Ibid.*, p. 55.

Added to these general considerations concerning the subordination of Christ's authority to the authority of Scripture is the more specific argument from His stated purpose in relation to the Scriptures.

The purpose of His mission: "All ultimate authority rests in God."[9] Christ recognized that ultimately final authority rests in God when He said, ". . . my meat is to do the will of him that sent me, and to accomplish his work" (John 4:34; cf. 9:4). The general purpose then of Christ's mission to earth was to do the Father's will, whatever that included.

More specifically defining His own relation to the will of the Father already recorded in the Old Testament He said: "Think not that I came to destroy the law or the prophets: I came not to destroy but to fulfill. For verily I say unto you, Till heaven and earth pass away one jot or one tittle shall in no wise pass away from the law, till all things be accomplished" (Matt. 5:17-18).

We have seen that this passage declares the divine unity and indestructibility of Scripture. It also declares the supreme and divine authority of Christ. Since He came to fulfil the Law and the Prophets and thus identified Himself with them it is clear that they are authoritative and binding.

The submission of the authoritative Christ to the authority of Scripture might also be illustrated from the six apparent antitheses recorded in the Sermon on the Mount. It was established earlier that Christ's "Ye have heard . . . but I say unto you" in no way militated against the authority of Scripture. It will not be necessary to present those arguments again here. The words of Stonehouse serve as a fitting reminder of Christ's acceptance of the authority of Scripture even in the Sermon on the Mount where there seems to be an impingement of Scripture by His "but I say unto you." "The sovereignty with which Jesus speaks is so absolute and unequivocal that his fulfillment of the law seems to carry with it the invalidation of the law of Moses. In the light of Jesus' categorical affirmation of the validity of the law and the prophets which immediately precedes the antithesis and of his decisive use of the authority of the Scriptures in controversy, however, it would be rash to conclude, without the most care-

---

[9] F. Norval Geldenhuys, "Authority and the Bible," *Revelation and the Bible*, ed. Carl F. H. Henry (Grand Rapids: Baker Book House, 1958), p. 375.

ful scrutiny of Jesus' words, that he actually meant to abrogate the authority of the law."[10]

Concluding this section then it may be well to be reminded that there is a unique relationship between the authority of Christ and the authority of the Old Testament in His teaching. Neither authority abrogates the other in any sense. His emphasis upon His own authority did not set aside the authority of the Scriptures; neither did His teaching of the authority of Scripture set aside His own authority. There is a divine harmony between the two and the one is disclosed in the other. Packer stated it succinctly when he said: "The question, 'What think ye of the Old Testament? ' resolves into the question, 'What think ye of Christ?' and our answer to the first proclaims our answer to the second. . . . To undercut Christ's teaching about the authority of the Old Testament is to strike at His own authority at the most fundamental point."[11]

The divine authority of the Old Testament and the divine authority of Christ confirm each other so that it is impossible to accept the one and not the other. In fact not to accept both of them would be to accept neither of them. This is true because He placed the Old Testament on a level of truth, authority and perpetuity with His own words when He declared of both that heaven and earth would pass away before one word of either should fail (Matt. 5:18; 24:35).

The Authority of the Old Testament

There are many ways by which the authority of the Old Testament could be proven from Christ's teaching. The arguments presented thus far most certainly lead to that conclusion. Christ's use of Scripture and His teaching of the origination and inspiration of Scripture lead inevitably to its authority. If the Scriptures come from God they are inspired by Him and if they are inspired by Him they are authoritative. This logical deduction is bolstered by the many explicit passages in which Christ states clearly His confidence in the authority of the Scriptures.

In addition to the proofs presented thus far for Christ's teaching of the authority of the Old Testament there re-

---

[10] Ned Bernard Stonehouse, *The Witness of Matthew and Mark to Christ* (Philadelphia: The Presbyterian Guardian, 1944), p. 199.

[11] Packer, *op. cit.*, pp. 59-61.

mains to be considered His teaching of the canonicity and historicity of Scripture and His unmistakable teaching of its authority in John 10:34, 35. The acceptance of the limits of the canon and the historical accuracies of the Old Testament account are necessary essentials to any true view of the authority of Scripture. If the canon is not closed and confined to the books contained in the Bible then it cannot be the only and final authority. Likewise, if the historical portions are not accounts of factual happenings which actually took place as recorded, the authority of Scripture cannot be accepted.

Christ's teaching of the canonicity and historicity of Scripture as these relate to authority will now be considered.

Canonicity and authority

The material to be included here will be brief since the purpose is not to exhaust the subject of canonicity but merely to consider Christ's teaching on the subject. Only such general considerations will be included which are necessary to fully understand His teaching on the subject.

The meaning of canonicity: The word "canon" comes from the Greek word "kanon" which was probably borrowed from the Hebrew word "kaneh." It means a reed or a measured rod. It came to mean a rule of faith and later a catalogue or list. Thus to speak of the canonicity of Scripture is to speak of the collection of inspired writings in the Bible.

Canonicity has to do with the recognition and collection of the inspired books which came from God and are thus authoritative and deserving of a place in the Holy Scripture. A distinction must be maintained between the canonicity and the authority of the book. "Its canonicity is dependent upon its authority. For when we ascribe canonicity to a book we simply mean that it belongs to the canon or list. . . . People frequently speak and write as if the authority with which the books of the Bible are invested in the minds of Christians is the result of their having been included in the sacred list. But the historical fact is the other way about; they were and are included in the list because they were acknowledged as authoritative."[12]

---

[12] F. F. Bruce, *The Books and the Parchments* (London: Pickering and Inglis Ltd., 1950), pp. 94-95.

The acceptance of the books of the Old Testament by Christ, the Jews and the church did not therefore impart inspiration and thus authority upon them. They were accepted because they were inspired and therefore authoritative.

The canon of the Jews of Christ's day: It is a commonly acknowledged fact that the Old Testament was divided by the Jews into three parts of twenty-four books. The 24-book division is as follows:

First: *The Law* (5 books)
Genesis, Exodus, Leviticus, Numbers, Deuteronomy

Second: *The Prophets* (8 books)

1. The Former Prophets (4 books)
   Joshua, Judges, Samuel, Kings
2. The Latter Prophets (4 books)
   (1) Major (3 books)
   Isaiah, Jeremiah, Ezekiel
   (2) Minor (1 book) The Twelve:
   Hosea, Joel, Amos, Obadiah, Jonah, Micah, Nahum, Habakkuk, Zephaniah, Haggai, Zechariah, Malachi

Third: *The Writings* (11 books)

1. Poetical (3 books)
   Psalms, Proverbs, Job
2. Five Rolls (5 books)
   Song, Ruth, Lamentations, Ecclesiastes, Esther
3. Historical (3 books)
   Daniel, Ezra-Nehemiah, Chronicles

This 24-book threefold division was generally accepted. There is evidence from Josephus (37-103 A.D.), Jerome (340-420), and a few others that there was also a threefold division of twenty-two books. This numbering was arrived at, however, by a rearranging of the same number of books.

It is not certain when the Jews began to refer to their Scriptures in this threefold way; neither is it pertinent to the discussion at hand. What is pertinent is that the number of books considered canonical was the same whether in a twofold or threefold division. Actually, the New Testament writers do not maintain a rigidity of designation in their reference to the Old Testament.[13] Sometimes the Old Testament is referred to as "law," "law and prophets," "scripture" and sometimes as "law, prophets and psalms." There is evidence of an early threefold division however. "The Prologue to Ecclesiasticus in the second century B.C. refers to the Old Testament in this way. Josephus and Philo refer to the books in this manner, and Jesus Christ also in Luke 24:44 . . . ."[14]

On the basis of the objective historical evidence then, it may be concluded that the canon of the Jews of Christ's day included all the books of the Old Testament and no more. The following summary by G. Douglas Young is to the point: "No reason exists for believing that the collection of books thus referred to by Christ and considered as Scripture by him differed in any particular from the collection of the Jews. There is no evidence of any dispute between him and the Jews on this point. Christ opposed the Pharisees, not over the identity of the canonical books but because their oral tradition made the Canon void. The statements of Josephus and Philo make it clear that they also recognized this threefold distinction. By comparing Josephus and the later Talmud and other sources, such as Melito the Bishop of Sardis (170 A.D.), we may learn the names of all the books of the three groups in the Jewish Canon of the day of Christ. These

[13] R. Laird Harris, *Inspiration and Canonicity of the Bible* (Grand Rapids: Zondervan Publishing House, 1957), pp. 141-53, gives an excellent discussion favoring a twofold division. He cites evidence from the Talmud, Josephus and the Dead Sea literature related to the community of Qumran. His view maintains the integrity of the New Testament writers and spells doom on the three-stage canonization theory.

[14] G. Douglas Young, "The Apocrypha," *Revelation and the Bible*, ed. Carl F. H. Henry (Grand Rapids: Baker Book House, 1958), p. 180.

The Septuagint version, which is a Greek translation of the Old Testament dating about 250 B.C.-160 B.C., contains the Apocryphal books in addition to the twenty-four books of the Hebrew canon. Because of the inclusion of these books along with the canonical books in the Septuagint some have advanced the idea of the existence of two canons. The appeal is made that the Jews in Egypt where the Septuagint was made held these extra books in high esteem. It is also claimed that some of the early Christians also honored them. On the contrary Josephus limits the canon to twenty-two books which books were probably arranged to agree with the number of letters in the Hebrew alphabet but consisted of the thirty-nine now in the Old Testament.

are 24 in number, the same books numbering 39 in our Old Testament Canon."[15]

The canon of Christ: It can be assuredly claimed and unquestionably proved that Christ accepted the Hebrew canon or Old Testament, excluded all other literatures as inspired, and allowed for the New Testament canon in His teaching.

Christ's acceptance of the Hebrew canon and all the books included in it was stated specifically and clearly by Him in two passages and implied in many others.

The first clear passage to be considered in which He refers to the canon is Matthew 23:35. The pronouncement of woes upon the scribes and Pharisees by Christ included His prophecy of death for some of His prophets so that upon the scribes and Pharisees the guilt of their murderous crimes might be poured out. Christ said, ". . . that upon you may come all the righteous blood shed on the earth, from the blood of Abel the righteous unto the blood of Zachariah son of Barachiah, whom ye slew between the sanctuary and the altar" (Matt. 23:35; cf. Luke 11:51). This all-inclusive reference, from the first to the last book of the Hebrew canon, lends support to the fact that the third section—the Writings or Psalms—contained all the books it now contains. Bruce observes: "It is almost certain that the Bible with which He was familiar ended with the books of Chronicles, which comes right at the end of the 'Writings' in the Hebrew Bible. . . . Now Abel is obviously the first martyr of the Bible, but why should Zachariah come last? Because in the order of books in the Hebrew Bible he is the last martyr to be named; in 2 Chron. 24:21 we read how he was stoned while he prophesied to the people in the court of the house of the Lord."[16]

---

[15] *Ibid.*, p. 181.

[16] Bruce, *op. cit.*, p. 96. A problem exists in the reference to Zacharias by Christ. The passage in II Chronicles, to which Christ apparently makes mention, speaks of Zechariah as the son of Jehoiada rather than the son of Barachias, which is the New Testament statement. Lange lists several possible explanations for this difficulty (*Commentary on the Holy Scriptures*, VIII, 414-15. C. F. Keil also acknowledges the difference in the names of the fathers but still attributes Christ's reference to the II Chronicles 24 murder. (*Chronicles*, p. 418). Gaussen, in his classic, *The Plenary Inspiration of the Holy Scriptures*, also gives a detailed explanation of the difficulty (pp. 237-41).

Thus in a somewhat incidental way, while warning the scribes and Pharisees of impending judgment, Christ gave His consent to the existing Old Testament canon.

There is another passage which with equal force presents Christ's acceptance of the extent of the Old Testament of His day. The words were spoken by Him after his resurrection and thus confirm the consistent view which He held. When He appeared in the upper room in Jerusalem after His conversation to the two on the road to Emmaus, in which He began with Moses and through all the prophets interpreted to them things concerning Himself (Luke 24:27), He said to the disciples, ". . . These are my words which I spake unto you, while I was yet with you, that all things must needs be fulfilled, which are written in the law of Moses, and the prophets, and the psalms, concerning me" (Luke 24:44). Here is a clear recognition of the three divisions of the Old Testament as well as a divine claim that the things written therein must be fulfilled.

It is an almost universally accepted fact that "law of Moses" refers to the first five books of the Old Testament and that the "prophets" includes the historical books and those of the writing prophets. There is difference of opinion, however, over the meaning of "psalms" as used by Christ. Many accept it as a reference to all the books in the third division of the canon. Others refer it only, in the instance cited above, to the book of Psalms.[17] In either case the fact remains that what Christ was here accepting was what the Jews had accepted as canonical. The point of importance is not the number of divisions but the identity of the books included in the canon regardless of the number of divisions.

Again, G. Douglas Young's comment is well taken: "Thus the collection of books in the Jewish Canon grew up gradually over the period of years during which they were being composed. But all Jews accepted only 24 books, our 39, as Scripture. Those 24 books include none of the Apocryphal books. This was the Canon of the Jews at the time of Christ,

---

[17] Edward J. Young, "The Authority of the Old Testament," *The Infallible Word*, ed. N. B. Stonehouse and Paul Wooley (Grand Rapids: Wm. B. Eerdmans Publishing Co., 1953), p. 58.

the Canon which he accepted, the Canon of the Christian church."[18]

In addition to these two central passages there are many other references which present Christ's total acceptance of the complete Hebrew canon. On many occasions He referred to the whole Old Testament as "law," "law and prophets," and "scripture." Also, He promised to fulfil "all the scriptures" and He said, ". . . one jot or one tittle shall in no wise pass from the law, till all things be accomplished" (Matt. 5:18). It is true that these and similar titles do not define the limits of the Old Testament canon. However, it is also true that they do most definitely assume the existence of a complete and separate collection of sound writings.

Thus far the positive arguments in favor of the accepted canonical Scriptures have been presented. What of the Apocryphal books which were not considered canonical but were included in the Septuagint version? Did Christ ever quote from these? The answer to this latter question is a categorical no. Christ's complete silence regarding the non-canonical writings has been alluded to earlier and the point need not be labored here.

Not only was Christ completely silent with regard to the Apocryphal books, but He was also silent concerning any criticism of His contemporaries regarding their accepted canon. "He never charges them with adding to or taking from the Scriptures, or in any way tampering with the text. Had they been guilty of so great a sin it is hardly possible that among the charges brought against them, this matter should not even be alluded to. . . . He never hints that they have foisted any book into the canon, or rejected any which deserved a place in it."[19]

The didactic ministry of Christ not only reveals His acceptance of the Old Testament canon of the Jews and of the present time, but also clearly allows for the New Testament canon. Since all the New Testament books were not in existence until about one hundred years after Christ's death He could not put His divine imprimatur upon them as He did

[18] G. Douglas Young, *Revelation and the Bible*, p. 180.

[19] William Caven, "The Testimony of Christ to the Old Testament," *The Fundamentals* (Chicago: Testimony Publishing Company, n.d.), IV, 47.

the Old Testament books. This in no way implies that we accept the New Testament on a lesser authority than we do the Old Testament. Actually, when the facts are examined it is discovered that the Saviour who accepted the authority of the Old Testament is the Saviour who anticipated the authority of the New.

From the multitude of disciples which followed Jesus He chose twelve whom He called apostles (Luke 6:12f.). The word "apostles" means "to send forth" and connotes the idea of purpose in the sending. Thus when Christ sent out His apostles they were not merely sent as messengers but as messengers with a special commission and as commissioners of the Christ who sent them forth. They were to be His delegates and were to teach and act in His name and on the basis of His authority (Matt. 10:5ff.).

The Gospel of John is especially clear regarding Christ's promise to send the Holy Spirit who would give the apostles the necessary equipment for their high calling, which was paralleled only by the calling of the Old Testament prophets (John 15:25f.; 16:18-23). The twofold promise of John 14:26 is a clear indication of the Lord's promise to provide guidance and remembrance to the apostles through the Holy Spirit.

Christ's acceptance of the Hebrew canon of Scripture did not imply the cessation of further special revelation from God. In fact He told the apostles there would be more truth to come and thus He recognized that the canon was not closed (John 16:13). The content of the words which the apostles wrote and their claims of authority testify to the fulfillment of Christ's promise to them. "But it is a remarkable fact that there is no teaching in the New Testament which is not already present in principle in the teaching of Jesus Himself. The apostles did not add to His teaching; under the guidance of the promised Spirit they interpreted and applied it."[20]

Concerning the canon of Christ the case may be stated plainly. He wholeheartedly accepted the Hebrew canon of the Jews which consisted of the thirty-nine books in the Old Testament. He never quoted or even referred to any of the noncanonical books in any authoritative way. Finally, though He could not place His approval and acceptance upon the New

---

[20] Bruce, *op. cit.*, pp. 104-5.

Testament canon as He did upon the Old, His teaching allows for the New and promises the same divine Spirit in its construction as had borne men along to write the Old. Thus the same authority which was invested in the Old Testament and claimed by Christ for Himself was promised for the New Testament.

Historicity and authority

The authority of Scripture in Christ's teaching relates as much to the historicity of Scripture as it does to the canonicity of Scripture. Here we want to show the extent to which Christ endorsed the authority of the Scriptures. He not only accepted the authority of the canon as a whole but He also rested in the authority of many of the historical accounts in the Old Testament.

Christ's reference to historical circumstances: These are many and varied and reveal the extensive knowledge and use which Christ had of the Old Testament. They also reveal His endorsement of the validity of Old Testament history. W. E. Vine has arranged a list of some of the significant references to historical happenings in Christ's teaching. The list will be included here to set forth the extensive use which Christ made of Old Testament history (page 98).

This list is representative and suggestive of the extensive use which Christ made of the historical circumstances recorded in the Old Testament.

A study of all the instances in which Christ refers to historical facts reveals that He included many things. He speaks of narratives, individuals, institutions and many miscellaneous items in His usage. His references to these circumstances, no matter what their classification may be, authenticates the historicity of the incidents referred to. Not only that, but His citations of these historical events also places His divine stamp of approval upon the authenticity of the events and the authority of the record which contains them. Many of Christ's quotations and references to historical events were given as illustrations of some teaching of His and often they were associated with divine retribution because of sin.

Christ's Reference to Historical Circumstances

	Recorded in	New Testament
The creation of man,	Gen. 5.2	Matt.19.4
The murder of Abel,	Gen. 4	Matt. 23.35
The times of Noah,	Gen. 7	Matt. 24.37
The Flood,	Gen. 7	Luke 17.27
The days of Lot,	Gen. 13	Luke 17.28
The destruction of Sodom,	Gen. 19	Luke 17.29
The Word of God to Moses,	Exod. 3.6	Matt. 22.32
The rite of circumcision,	Gen. 17.10	John 7.22
The giving of the Law,	Exod. 20	John 7.19
The commandments of the Law,	Exod. 20.12-16	Matt. 19.18
The ceremonial law *re* leprosy,	Lev. 14	Mark 1.44
The lifting up of the serpent of brass,	Num. 21.9	John 3.14
The profanation of the temple by the priests,	see Num. 28.9, 10; 1 Chron. 9.30-32	Matt. 12.5
David's eating of the shewbread,	1 Sam. 21	Matt. 12.3
The glory of Solomon,	1 Kings 10	Matt. 6.29
The Queen of Sheba's visit to Solomon,	1 Kings 10	Matt. 12.42
The famine in the days of Elijah,	1 Kings 17	Luke 4.25
The sending of Elijah to a widow in Sidon,	1 Kings 17	Luke 4.25
The healing of Naaman by Elisha,	2 Kings 5	Luke 4.27
The stoning of Zechariah,	2 Chron. 24.21	Matt. 23.35
Daniel's prophecy of the abomination of desolation,	Dan. 9.27, etc.	Matt. 24.15
Jonah's message to Nineveh,	Jonah 3.5	Matt. 12.41[21]

[21] W. E. Vine, *The Divine Inspiration of the Bible* (London: Pickering & Inglis, 1923), pp. 38-39.

Summarizing Christ's attitude toward the historical narratives of the Old Testament Wenham states: "Although these quotations are taken by our Lord more or less at random from different parts of the Old Testament and some periods of the history are covered more fully than others, it is evident that He was familiar with most of our Old Testament and that He treated it all equally as history. Curiously enough, the narratives that proved least acceptable to what was known a generation or two ago as 'the modern mind' are the very ones that He seemed most fond of choosing for His illustrations."[22]

The significance of Christ's references: It may be argued by some that Christ's use of the Old Testament stories does not necessitate His belief in their unimpeachable history. Legends and allegories may be used to illustrate spiritual truth without implying an acceptance of their historicity.

All possibility of such a usage by Christ evaporates when the way in which Christ used these historical narratives is studied and when it is seen that the entire validity of His arguments stands or falls upon the actual objective historicity of the events He refers to.

Most of the passages in which Christ makes reference to historical happenings will admit of no other than an historical interpretation. Matthew records the words of Christ in Matthew 12:41 concerning the men of Nineveh: "The men of Nineveh shall stand up in the judgment with this generation, and shall condemn it: for they repented at the preaching of Jonah; and behold, a greater than Jonah is here." Intellectual honesty demands that any interpretation which sees this as imaginary preaching by an imaginary prophet to imaginary people who repented in imagination must be rejected.

The reminder of the similarity of the days of Noah and the coming of the Son of Man introduces a reference to a whole period of history (Matt. 24:37). That the validity of Christ's argument depends upon the historicity of the events of the days of Noah is amplified by His unqualified assertion that "Heaven and earth shall pass away, but my words shall not pass away" (Matt. 24:35). Christ's declaration is not made effective here by mere reference to an unreal illustration but by reference to the historicity of the awful judging acts of

[22] J. W. Wenham, *Our Lord's View of the Old Testament* (London: The Tyndale Press, 1953), p. 9.

God. If Noah and the conditions in his day were not real neither is Christ or the conditions He predicted real.

From these examples it is obvious that the significance of Christ's references to these many historical events lies in the evident authority which He associated with them since upon many of them He based the validity of His own person and preaching. Having established the supreme and absolute authority of Christ it is a self-evident fact that what He says is true and a straightforward record of facts.

John 10:34-35 and authority

Christ claimed to be God and the Jews were about to stone Him. He defended Himself in the following manner: "Jesus answered them, Is it not written in your law, I said, Ye are gods? If he called them gods, unto whom the word of God came (and the scripture cannot be broken), say ye of him, whom the Father sanctified and sent into the world, Thou blasphemest; because I said, I am the Son of God?" (John 10:34-36). This passage declares with clarity and decisiveness the validity, indissolubleness and inviolability of Scripture.

Circumstances evoking the passage: Christ's claim to be the good shepherd (John 10:11) and the one who was invested with the power to lay down and take again His life (John 10:18) caused division among the Jews (John 10:19). That which infuriated them above all else was His claim to be equal with the Father (John 10:30). At this stupendous claim they took up stones to stone Him. The Jews recognized His divine claim and charged Him with blasphemy. The charge of blasphemy was a serious one. The Greek word translated blasphemy means "to speak evil of someone" and is usually translated "blaspheme" and sometimes "defame" or "speak evil of." The Jews acknowledged Christ's claim for what it really was—a claim to be God.

The Lord's reply, however, begins with an appeal on their grounds and their law. He found fault with their basic premise by referring them to Psalm 82:6.

At first glance Christ's defense may be thought to be inadequate; yet it was sufficient to repel the charge of blasphemy. Christ certainly made Himself God in a far higher sense than the judges of Israel had ever done or could ever do. The essence of His reply is that if the spiritual judges among Israel could be called "gods" without blasphemy then certainly the Son of God whom the Father sent into the world had a right to that designation.

Meaning and significance of the passage: There are two phrases in these verses which are pertinent to Christ's teaching of the authority of Scripture. The purpose of Christ stated here was to attribute to the Scripture the very authority of God.

The first phrase is in the form of a question, ". . . Is it not written in your law, I said, Ye are gods?" (John 10:34). It is immediately apparent that Christ's defense takes the form of an appeal to Scripture. The appeal is to that which was "written." Thus He refers to propositional words and not mere oral tradition or concepts. Too, He adduces the Scripture as that which possesses legal and divine authority—"law." The significant fact is that the passage which He quotes is from Psalm 82:6 and not in the Law or Pentateuch section of Scripture. Warfield's observation is well stated: "It is written in the Book of Psalms; and in a particular psalm which is as far as possible from presenting the external characteristics of legal enactment (Ps. lxxxii.6). When Jesus adduces this passage, then, as written in the 'law' of the Jews, He does it, not because it stands in this psalm, but because it is a part of Scripture at large. In other words, He here ascribes legal authority to the entirety of Scripture, in accordance with a conception common enough among the Jews (cf. Jn. xii. 34). . . ."[23]

In addition to the importance of His reference to Scripture as written law the quotation "I said, Ye are gods" is also important. By His use of these words from Psalm 82 He is not only singling out a particular verse which He viewed as authoritative but He hangs the validity of His entire argument upon one word of that verse. That word is "gods." This one word which He calls written law and Scripture is that which cannot be annulled. Upon this one word He defends His claim to be the Son of God. The conclusion is obvious that if one single word cannot be annulled then certainly the whole of Scripture possesses the same divine authority.

[23] Benjamin Breckinridge Warfield, *The Inspiration and Authority of the Bible* (Philadelphia: The Presbyterian and Reformed Publishing Company, 1948), pp. 138-39.

The second phrase of special significance to Christ's teaching of the authority of Scripture is ". . . and the scripture cannot be broken" (John 10:35). This statement was made somewhat as a reply by the Lord to His own question. The reason it was worthwhile to appeal to what was written in their law is because that law is Scripture and the Scripture cannot be broken. Edward J. Young has succinctly summarized the importance of the word "scripture" here: "The force of his argument is very clear, and may be paraphrased as follows: 'What is stated in this verse from the Psalms is true because this verse belongs to that body of writings known as Scripture, and the Scripture possesses an authority so absolute in character that *it cannot be broken.*' When Christ here employs the word Scripture, he has in mind, therefore, not a particular verse in the Psalms, but rather the entire group of writings of which this one verse is a part."[24]

Christ here plainly equates "law" and "scripture" and uses these terms as strict synonyms. His appeal to law as Scripture is made all the more certain by the highly emphatic phrase "and the scripture cannot be broken," which simply means it is irrefragable and inerrant.

The word "cannot" expresses a divine and moral impossibility. The point is, Scripture cannot be annulled, dissolved, abrogated or rendered void because it declares the will and purpose of God. Of equal importance in Christ's statement is the word "broken." By this expression He emphasizes not only the divine authority but also the unity and solidarity of Scripture. What cannot happen to one minute part cannot happen to the whole.

Warfield's statement on the word "broken" as used in John 10:35 is apropos here: "The word 'broken' here is the common one for breaking the law, or the Sabbath, or the like (Jn. v.18; vii.23; Mt. v.19), and the meaning of the declaration is that it is impossible for the Scripture to be annulled, its authority to be withstood, or denied. . . . What we have here is, therefore, the strongest possible assertion of the indefectible authority of Scripture; precisely what is true of Scripture is that it 'cannot be broken.' . . . This means, of course, that in the Saviour's view the indefectible authority of

---

[24] Edward J. Young, *The Infallible Word,* p. 55.

Scripture attaches to the very form of expression of its most casual clauses."[25]

The significance of these words of Christ is evident from the discovery of their meaning. His words silenced His critics not because they suddenly accepted His authority but because He met their accusation of Him on their own grounds, namely, their law. There is a vein of satire running through the conversation but it will not do to dismiss Christ's damaging blow to the Jews' argument and decisive and unqualified acclamation of the authority of Scripture as merely an *ad hominem* argument. The fact remains that the authoritative regard for Scripture displayed by Christ here is not an isolated example of His view. The first words He is recorded to have uttered (Matt. 4:4, 7, 10) and among the last He spoke to His disciples (Luke 24:44) are illustrative of His view of the indefectibility of Scripture.

For Christ then, the Scriptures were not only the communication of God to man and thus the very inspired words of God in their original proclamation but their origination and resultant inspiration gave them divine authority which could not be set at naught or annulled, reaching from the minutest detail to the entire gamut of God's declarations.

---

[25] Warfield, *op. cit.*, pp. 139-40.

Chapter V

CONTEMPORARY DENIALS OF THE SAVIOUR'S TEACHING

PART I, NEO-ORTHODOXY

The preceding chapters have established several important conclusions with regard to Christ's teaching about the Scriptures. It has been discovered that He used the Old Testament often under many circumstances and always treated it as the very Word of God. The fact that Scripture was revealed by God and thus originated with Him was also clearly taught by the Lord. He accepted and taught verbal plenary inspiration and thus total inerrancy of Scripture. The last chapter developed the unquestionable teaching of Christ concerning the absolute and supreme authority of Scripture. Thus, He presented a rather complete doctrine of the Scriptures in His ministry and that without ever having been asked by friend or foe concerning His view.

The call for a return to "Biblical theology" and a more "Christocentric theology" on the part of elements of contemporary theology demands an investigation into the kind of Bible and Christ which is being presented. How do the modern liberal and neo-orthodox views of Scripture compare with Christ's view? The present chapter dealing with the neo-orthodox view is divided into three major divisions which comprise the major areas of differentiation with Christ's view. After a brief discussion of the historical background, the neo-orthodox view of history, revelation, inspiration and authority, as these relate to Scripture, will be presented and compared with Christ's view.

THE HISTORICAL ORIENTATION

Orthodox church doctrine of Scripture

Though some have denied that the church ever held a doctrine of Scripture and though the doctrine has never received exhaustive historical treatment, the fact remains that the inerrancy of Scripture was held by the majority in Christendom until the rise of the naturalistic rationalism and mysticism of the eighteenth and nineteenth centuries. This fact is admitted by Cadoux. He accepts this fact when he says that the inerrancy of "Scripture . . . was accepted by Christendom with practical unanimity from the second century to the nineteenth."[1] James Orr who held an extremely high view of Scripture yet did not believe in verbal inerrancy frankly admitted the historic view of the church was on the side of inerrancy. "On this broad, general ground the advocates of 'inerrancy' may always feel that they have *a strong position*, whatever assaults may be made on them in matters of lesser detail. They stand undeniably, in their main contention, in the line of apostolic belief, and of the general faith of the Church, regarding Holy Scripture."[2]

This investigation will demonstrate the extent of the denial of this church doctrine within neo-orthodoxy.

Orthodox church doctrine discarded

The demise began with the introduction of rationalistic philosophy. The Renaissance (1453-1690), the Enlightenment (1690-1781) and the Idealistic (1781-1831) periods of rationalistic and idealistic developments paved the way for a complete rejection of the Bible as the supernatural and authoritative revelation of God.

The discarding of the church doctrine was further enhanced by Schleiermacher's introduction of a theology of feeling. Schleiermacher (1768-1834) founded his authority in the soul's experiences rather than in the Bible. In a day when the rationalism and materialism of the Renaissance were smashing damaging blows to historic Christianity, he

---

[1] Cecil John Cadoux, *The Case for Evangelical Modernism* (London: Hodder & Stoughton, 1938), p. 64.

[2] James Orr, *Revelation and Inspiration* (London: Duckworth & Co., 1910), pp. 216-17.

introduced a new approach to the understanding of religion. As a mediating theologian, he rejected the cold rationalism of the philosophers before him; yet he did not return to historic Christianity. Indeed, he introduced a theology of feeling which did not begin with the Bible but with the feeling of absolute dependence. For him true Christianity was not revealed in a set of propositions and dogmas to which a believer must subscribe, and to which the church had subscribed, but by an inner experience.

Thus it is seen that with the introduction of Schleiermacher's concept the emphasis shifted from the rationalistic basis of authority to a mystical basis. This subjective basis of authority merely transferred the source of authority from the intellect to the emotions. Neither of these sources are to be trusted because they both reside in man and man is fallible. Whereas the orthodox church doctrine exalted God's revelation in the Bible as the ultimate source of authority, the philosophers and later Schleiermacher found the ultimate source of authority in man's mind and in his emotions.

The steps from Schleiermacher to the present are not hard to trace. Philosophical theologians such as Hegel, Ritschl, Paulus, Baur, Strauss, Wellhausen, Harnack and Herrmann propagated the viewpoints of their forefathers and by so much rejected the church doctrine of the Scriptures.[3]

The forces which served to discredit the authoritative view of Scripture held by Christ and the church also served to introduce theological liberalism with its candid rejection of an infallible Bible. This old type of liberalism held sway in Europe until World War I shattered the optimistic outlook which had characterized its leaders. At the same time and with equal damage Karl Barth's neo-orthodoxy spelled doom to the humanistic approach which old liberalism had taken.

Thus, with the failure of old liberalism came the introduction of neo-orthodoxy with its repudiation of the exalted view of man which the liberal had taken. Also, arising from the ruins of old liberalism came a remade liberalism with determination to accommodate itself to the prevailing circumstances while at the same time to hold fast to the proposed gains which the old liberals had achieved.

---

[3] See Robert Lightner, *Neo-Liberalism* (Chicago: Regular Baptist Press, 1959), pp. 19-28.

The term *neo-orthodoxy* designates an attempt to be a mediating theology between orthodoxy and liberalism. The teachings of the system were introduced by Karl Barth even though he did not so name it. The men who espouse the system accept liberalism's foundation of the higher criticism of the Bible; thus it is rooted in the "gains" of classic liberalism. The name implies a relation to orthodoxy; yet the only essential agreement which its exponents have with orthodoxy is the use of orthodox terminology. The crucial disagreement lies in the new meanings with which neo-orthodox men have invested those terms.

A formal definition is difficult to formulate; yet the movement has characteristics which can be identified. It is that ". . . movement which began early in the twentieth century as a reaction against the optimistic view of man which the liberal had taken. While it is built on liberalism's view of the Bible it claims to be a return to orthodoxy. It is characterized by an emphasis upon the subjective experience of man as a criterion of truth. Neo-orthodoxy is sometimes called: Crisis Theology, Barthianism, Theology of Feeling and Neo-Supernaturalism."[4]

It was the introduction of this dialectical and mystical system of theology by Karl Barth and later by Emil Brunner, Reinhold Niebuhr and others which forced classic liberalism to be remade.

James Orr with discerning insight anticipated the present importance and concern over the doctrine of Scripture. At the beginning of this century he said regarding the task of theology in the century before him: "That battle will have to be fought, if I mistake not, in the first instance, round the fortress of the worth and authority of Holy Scripture. A doctrine of Scripture adapted to the needs of the hour in harmonizing the demands at once of science and of faith, is perhaps the most clamant want at present in theology. But the whole conception of Christianity will get drawn in, and many of the old controversies will be reviewed in new forms."[5]

The accuracy of Orr's prediction will be evident from the discussion which follows.

---

[4] Robert Lightner, *Neo-Evangelicalism* (Findlay, Ohio: The Dunham Publishing Co., 1962), pp. 17-18.

[5] James Orr, *The Progress of Dogma* (New York: A. C. Armstrong & Son, 1902), pp. 352-53.

The Neo-Orthodox View of Scripture

Because of the significant part which neo-orthodoxy played in the outmoding of classic liberalism and the remaking of new liberalism first consideration will be given to the determinative views of Scripture among the neo-orthodox. The view of history accepted by the neo-orthodox is of extreme importance in relation to their view of Scripture and will therefore receive immediate consideration.

History in relation to Scripture

The neo-orthodox concept of history is basic to their view of revelation, inspiration and authority. In fact their view of history is foundational to their entire theological structure. The concept of history which is endorsed by them makes it possible for them to speak of the doctrines of orthodoxy and yet not believe them as the orthodox do. Neo-orthodoxy does not accept the Christian interpretation of history and its view flatly contradicts Christ's view of the historicity of the Old Testament. The paradoxical element in the neo-orthodox concept of history and Scripture is that while its exponents claim to present a Christologically-orientated theology they reject the clear and authoritative claims of Christ.

Barthianism views history in a twofold light. Variations exist in the terms in which neo-orthodox men present their views but basically they all make a distinction between history which relates to fact and history which relates to event.

Historie and Geschichte: "By *Historie* Barth means history as studied by the average historian, whether Christian or non-Christian."[6] Sometimes there is an overlapping in the neo-orthodox view of *Historie* and *Geschichte*. There are crucial junctures, however, where the distinction is crucial to his view. *Historie* refers to the facts which are recordable and related to the creature. It is historiographic history as opposed to unhistoriographic history. The distinction between history and real history is usually made in the creation account and the account of the resurrection of Christ.

Neo-orthodoxy maintains that, when the Bible speaks of the creation of man, history as such is not in view. To the neo-orthodox, the so-called history of creation is pure saga.

---

[6] Cornelius Van Til, *Christianity and Barthianism* (Philadelphia: The Presbyterian and Reformed Publishing Co., 1962), pp. 8-9.

Barth admits that the resurrection appearances deal with facts which could be seen and felt but he refuses to directly identify the resurrection with any such fact. "The resurrection as *Historie* is only a subordinate aspect of the resurrection as *Geschichte*. The real relation between God and man takes place in terms of Christ as *Geschichte*."[7]

Another neo-orthodox term used in explaining its view of history is *primal history*. This is in contrast to real history. This means there is history behind history. The one operates on the plane of faith; the other on the plane of sight. Before the monuments become understandable and credible records appear, everything is in the realm of primal history and the plane of faith.

This concept of history did not originate with the neo-orthodox. It originated with the philosophy of Kant. According to Kant the doctrine of creation and the fall are not to be taken as referring to events that took place in time. The record of the temporal origin of creation and evil was to him metaphorical language. It was thus the philosophical as well as the theological background of neo-orthodoxy which helped to formulate its concept of history and consequently of Scripture.

Influence upon Scripture: Obviously this concept of history played havoc with the normal interpretation of historical happenings recorded in Scripture. While supposedly exalting and defending the sovereignty and hiddenness of God by this interpretation of history Barthians divest many of the Scriptural records of any ordinary historical meaning. They believe God's transcendence and greatness is lessened by attributing to God the creation of the world and man in time. Barth candidly states: "Adam has no existence on the plane of history and of psychological analysis."[8] Again he states concerning the sin which entered the world through Adam that it ". . . is in no strict sense an historical or psychological happening. . . . The sin which entered the world through Adam is like the righteousness manifested to the world in Christ, timeless and transcendental."[9] Concerning the res-

---

[7] *Ibid.*

[8] Karl Barth, *The Epistle to the Romans*, trans. from the 6th ed. by Edwyn C. Hoskyns (London: Oxford University Press, 1933), p. 171.

[9] *Ibid.*

urrection Barth says that in one sense ". . . the Resurrection is not an event in history at all."[10]

Thus the damaging effect of this view of history upon Scripture is inestimable. The historical bases for creation, Adam, the fall, and aspects of the life and death of Christ are stripped from the Scriptural record and these circumstances are removed to a so-called plane of faith. The neo-orthodox concept is foreign to the Biblical view. Young says: "The Bible knows nothing about any region or realm which, in distinction from the historical, is to be labeled faith, or redemption, or supra-temporal, or supra-historical, or *Urgeschichte*, or a realm where history and nature are inadequate. To put the matter baldly, it would seem that these are but new names for the old area of myth and legend."[11]

Relation to Christ's view: The view of history presented by the neo-orthodox is not only illogical and inconsistent with itself but it also contradicts the view of history which Christ presented. The comparison and contrast is abundantly evident when Christ's repeated references to historical events and personalities are reviewed.[12]

Christ's acceptance of the historicity of that which the Old Testament records leaves no room for the dual concept of history propounded by neo-orthodoxy. Never in any of His many references to the historic happenings recorded in the Old Testament does He even so much as hint that what was there recorded and what His contemporaries had accepted was anything but factual. He referred to persons, places, events, institutions and many happenings and never once did He take them in any other way than as actual historical circumstances.

There is not only disagreement between Christ's view and that of neo-orthodoxy but there is evident contradiction between the two views. As was discussed earlier in chapter four the validity of Christ's arguments depends upon the actual historicity of the facts referred to. Christ never accepted the historical facts He referred to in any other than a literal way and to say that He did is to charge Him with intended falsehood. Thus there is complete disagreement on

---

[10] *Ibid.*, p. 30.

[11] Edward J. Young, *Thy Word Is Truth* (Grand Rapids: Wm. B. Eerdmans Publishing Co., 1957), p. 251.

[12] See Chapter 4.

the part of neo-orthodoxy with the Christ it claims to exalt as the climactic revelation of God.

The contradiction is made even more obvious when it is realized that one of the very crucial areas in which Barthians reject the normal interpretation of history is the very area stressed by Christ as that which is purely historical in the ordinary sense of the word. Reference is here made to the Genesis account of creation. It has been shown that neo-orthodoxy views this account as beyond history, calling it primal history and an unhistoriographical "event."

Christ's appeal to the creation of man places His stamp of approval on passages in Genesis 1 and 2 (Matt. 19:4, 5; Mark 10:6-8). The Saviour said, "Have ye not read, that he which made them at the beginning made them male and female" (Matt. 19:4). Thus, He clearly ascribes the origin of the race to God as is recorded in Genesis 1. Adam was not a myth to the Saviour. Thus to speak of the creation of man in terms other than historical, in the ordinary understanding of the term, is to cast aspersions upon Christ, the very one whom neo-orthodoxy proposes to exalt and unite to creation.

Revelation in Scripture

Having considered the neo-orthodox view of history it is now appropriate to investigate the neo-orthodox view of revelation as it relates to Scripture. First in order is an understanding of the meaning of revelation in the framework of neo-orthodoxy. This will be followed by a presentation of the salient features in the neo-orthodox concept of revelation in Scripture.

Barth gives an etymological definition: "Revelation *(apokalypsis, phanerosis, epiphaneia)* really means here what the word implies, viz., the appearance of that which is new; the appearance, therefore, of that which is in no wise known before. That which is new is primarily Jesus Christ Himself, His person in its concrete *reality*."[13]

Weber's quotation of Barth is pertinent: "God's Word is God himself in his revelation. For God reveals himself as the Lord, and according to Scripture that means, for the concept of revelation, that God himself is the Revealer, the Revela-

[13] Karl Barth, "Revelation," *Revelation*, ed. John Baillie and Hugh Martin (London: Faber and Faber Limited, 1937), pp. 45-46.

tion and the Revealedness in indestructible unity, but also in indestructible distinction."[14]

Thus in the Barthian concept revelation is God revealing Himself as Lord It is the making known of God Himself, not the making known of facts about Himself. God, in the neo-orthodox concept, has not revealed propositions or truths about Himself but only Himself.

Emil Brunner agrees with the usual concept of revelation in neo-orthodox theology. He writes: "Finally all that has been said leads up to this point: the real content of revelation in the Bible is not 'something' but God Himself. Revelation is the self-manifestation of God."[15] In this same connection Brunner gives an extended treatment to the matter of revelation and his understanding of the Biblical concept. His entire discussion centers around revelation as that which is personal and concerns God Himself and not propositions about Him.

Combining the concepts presented above Witmer gives an objective formal definition of revelation in Barthian theology: ". . . revelation is the continuous personal activity of the infinite God, unveiling Himself through self-communication and the appearance of that which is new to men, confronting them with the divine imperative for the redemptive purpose of establishing a transforming fellowship with them."[16]

Revelation as personal: In opposition to revelation as propositional the neo-orthodox emphasize revelation as personal, centering in Christ.

The reason for this insistence of revelation as personal is because of the neo-orthodox belief that revelation is the self-manifestation of God and God is known primarily through Christ. The Scriptures therefore become a witness to the revelation of God in Christ. They are never the revelation of God *per se.*

---

[14] Otto Weber, *Karl Barth's Church Dogmatics,* trans. Arthur C. Cochrane (Philadelphia: Westminster Press, 1952), p. 35.

[15] Emil Brunner, *Revelation and Reason,* trans. Olive Wyon (Philadelphia: The Westminster Press, 1951), p. 25.

[16] John A. Witmer, "A Critical Study of Current Trends in Bibliology" (unpublished Th.D. dissertation, Dallas Theological Seminary, 1953), p. 191.

Revelation in events: Since revelation, in neo-orthodoxy, is not of propositional *truth* but always and only of a person then the method of that divine revelation must be limited to acts of God in nature, history, conscience and the human soul. This is precisely Brunner's concept. He writes: "In the time of the apostles, as in that of the Old Testament Prophets, divine revelation always meant the whole of the divine activity for the salvation of the world, the whole story of God's saving acts, of the 'acts' of God which reveal God's nature and His will, above all. . . . Divine revelation is not a book or a doctrine; the revelation is God Himself in His manifestation within history. Revelation is something that happens. . . ."[17]

A further word from Barth will confirm the present proposition. He writes concerning the relation of the Bible to revelation as follows: "It takes place as an event, i.e., when and where the word of the Bible functions as the word of a witness, when and where John's finger points not in vain but really pointedly, when and where by means of its word we also succeed in seeing and hearing what he saw and heard. Therefore, where the Word of God is an event, revelation and the Bible are one in fact, and word for Word one at that."[18]

Therefore, in this viewpoint there are no revealed commandments or doctrines in the Bible but merely revelatory events which are spoken of in doctrinal terms.

Revelation and response: The revelation of God in acts of history discussed above does not in itself or in the events constitute revelation *per se.* It is only revelation when God creates a subjective response to it in man.

"At this point the neo-orthodox theologians speak with unanimity. They all contend that revelation in order to be such must contain both an objective act of God and a subjective response by man."[19]

Neo-orthodoxy fails to present a uniform interpretation of the mighty revelatory acts of God in history. They do not even agree on the climactic revelation of God in Jesus Christ.

---

[17] Brunner, *op. cit.*, p. 8.

[18] Karl Barth, *Church Dogmatics*, Vol. I, Part I: *The Doctrine of the Word of God*, trans. G. T. Thomson (New York: Charles Scribner's Sons, 1936), p. 166.

[19] Kenneth Kantzer, "Revelation and Inspiration in Neo-Orthodox Theology," *Bibliotheca Sacra*, CXV (July, 1958), p. 220.

There are variations among them concerning His person. Acknowledging this fact Kantzer states: "Yet in their understanding of the nature and methods of revelation as such, these thinkers are essentially one. God reveals Himself, so they affirm with one voice, not in propositions but in mighty acts culminating in the supreme act of Jesus Christ; and these objective acts in order to be truly revelatory must be subjectively and personally appropriated by man."[20]

Revelation not in propositions of truth: The salient features presented above preclude the fact that the neo-orthodox view of revelation cancels any idea of revelation consisting in propositional sentences of truth.

William Temple stated the neo-orthodox concept plainly: "There is no such thing as revealed truth. These are truths of revelation, that is to say, propositions which express the results of correct thinking concerning revelation, but these are not themselves directly revealed. What is offered to man's apprehension in any specific revelation is not truth concerning God but the living God Himself."[21]

Barth, the most conservative of the neo-orthodox, does not speak of Scripture as the objective propositional record of the revelation of God. On the contrary he says, "Holy Scripture as such is not the revelation. . . . Holy Scripture is a *token* of revelation."[22] The identity of the Bible with revelation is in Barth's mind a fatal error. He views the Bible as fallible, thus containing errors and contradictions—a purely human book.

Baillie sums up the neo-orthodox view when he says: "From a very early time in the history of the church, the tendency had manifested itself to equate divine revelation with a body of information which God has communicated to man. We must rather think of Him as giving Himself to us in communion. Our examination of New Testament usage . . . amply confirms our conclusion that what is revealed is not a body of information or of doctrine. God does not give us information by communication, He gives us Himself in

---

[20] *Ibid.*, p. 223.

[21] William Temple, *Nature, Man and God* (London: The Macmillan Company, Ltd., 1954), p. 317.

[22] Barth, *Revelation*, p. 67.

communion. It is not information about God that is revealed but . . . God Himself."[23]

An even more recent exponent of neo-orthodoxy has put it this way: "God's Word never consists of black marks on the pages of a book called the Bible; God's Word is the living Word which he speaks through the Bible and to which man must respond by saying yes or no."[24]

Thus it can be seen that neo-orthodoxy presents a very different concept of revelation than that of the Bible and orthodoxy. Neo-orthodoxy views revelation as personal, in events, demanding a subjective response, as continuous and definitely not in propositions of truth. It remains to be seen how this view conflicts with Christ's view of revelation.

The neo-orthodox view compared with Christ's view: The teaching of Christ regarding the origination and revelation of Scripture has already been presented in chapter two of this discussion. The thesis established there, as the teaching of Christ, contradicts each one of the salient features of neo-orthodoxy's view of revelation presented above. Repetition of what He taught concerning revelation is not necessary here. It only needs to be demonstrated that His view differs drastically on each of the points discussed above.

Without question, Christ taught that Scripture was the revelation of God concerning His person and that the Law, the Prophets and the Psalms spoke of Him (Luke 24:27, 44). The record of John in chapter five is additional evidence that Christ saw the embodiment of Scripture in Himself. The point of contrast between His view and the neo-orthodox view, however, comes when it is seen that He pointed to the objective propositional writings of Moses and the prophets to show that revelation was personal. It was through what was written that the revelation of His person was revealed and without those written utterances knowledge of Him as the revelation of God would be impossible. His teaching and the teaching of the New Testament writers does not present an "either-or" concept regarding revelation as personal or propositional. It rather presents a "both-and" idea. God truly has revealed

---

[23] John Baillie, *The Idea of Revelation in Recent Thought* (New York: Columbia University Press, 1956), p. 29.

[24] William Hordern, *The Case for New Reformation Theology* (Philadelphia: The Westminster Press, 1959), p. 62.

Himself in the Word but He has done this by revealing facts, truths about Himself.

Christ had very little to say concerning the revelation of God in acts or events of history. By far His greatest emphasis was upon the record of those revelatory events deposited in the Scriptures. This is not to say that the God which Christ presented did not act but He also spoke and that which He challenged His hearers to obey was the propositional record of the acts of God. When intellectual honesty prevails the neo-orthodox must admit that a limitation of revelation to divine acts does not really fit the Biblical picture. The idea that revelation consists only of revelatory events is not Christ's view; it is the neo-orthodox view foisted upon the Bible. The neo-orthodox concept of God in revelation consists of a God who can act but cannot speak—a sort of "deaf-mute." On the contrary the God which Christ proclaimed is a God who can both act and speak and in fact has spoken concerning His actions through men in words in the Scriptures.

At no point is the neo-orthodox at greater variance with the Christ he claims to exalt than in the idea that revelation is really not revelation until there is a subjective response on the part of the one confronted with the Word. Christ did seek the response of His hearers to the Scriptures but their response or lack of it was in no way related to the inspiration and authority of that which stood written. The fact is that when Christ confronted His enemies with the Scriptures He did so because they had *refused to respond to it.* Their refusal to have an "encounter" (a neo-orthodox term) did not alter the fact that for Christ, His enemies, and everyone else, it still stood written and that settled the matter. There is not one shred of evidence to support the idea that Christ ever referred to the Scriptures as merely a witness to the revelation of God. For Him it was the Word of God written in propositions of truth and He appealed to it as final and incontrovertibly the written proclamation of God to those who accepted it as such and to those who refused to so accept it.

That Christ accepted Scripture as the Word of God whether it was subjectively received or not is clearly presented in Mark 7:6-18. Here He calls what Moses and Isaiah wrote "the commandment of God" and the "word of God" when it had obviously not been subjectively appropriated by those to whom He spoke. Thus, the human acceptance or response had absolutely nothing to do with the fact of its revelatory nature, inspiration, or authority. Again, in His reply to Satan during His temptation the issue was not that the Scripture witnessed to truth but that it stood written as truth even though Satan had obviously rejected its message.

It has been established that neo-orthodoxy views revelation as a continuous process. With this concept as with all the others neo-orthodoxy parts company with the very Christ it seeks to embrace. As was pointed out in chapter three Christ did make provision for the further revelation of the New Testament in His teaching. This, however, is not the point in controversy with neo-orthodoxy. The issue is: Did He teach as neo-orthodoxy does that the Scriptures become the Word of God to the individual at "moments" or times of "encounter" and that there is a continual process whereby the Bible now is the Word of God and again at another time it is not?

In contradistinction to this Christ taught that the Scriptures were the final court of appeal. Every reference of His to the written revelation of God is in blatant opposition to the idea of neo-orthodoxy that revelation is a continuous process.

Inspiration and authority of Scripture

There are differing views among neo-orthodox thinkers over the inspiration and authority of the Scriptures. All who are truly neo-orthodox reject the orthodox view but some treat the Scriptures with a great deal more respect than others. Karl Barth is perhaps the most orthodox of the neo-orthodox and therefore emphasis will be placed upon His views in the following discussion. If it can be determined that the most conservative of the neo-orthodox holds a view of inspiration which falls far short of the orthodox view and the view of Christ, then certainly those holding a more radical view fall short even more.

Confusion of revelation and inspiration: It will not be necessary to deal extensively with the neo-orthodox view of the inspiration of Scripture because what has been presented above as their view of revelation determines their view of inspiration.

It is a true axiom that one's view of revelation determines his view of inspiration and his view of inspiration in turn determines His view of the authority of Scripture. This fact is clearly illustrated in neo-orthodoxy. Therefore, the doctrines of inspiration and authority in neo-orthodoxy will be considered together. They are not synonymous but one's view of the former reveals his view of the latter. The neo-orthodox confusion of these doctrines is the result of the rejection of propositional revelation and thus requires a subjective human response before revelation becomes actual. Obviously, if truth has not been communicated it could certainly not be recorded.

Confusion of inspiration and illumination: Because neo-orthodoxy believes that the Word of God is made revelation to the individual by the ever-recurring act of God, whereby the Scriptures witness to the Word of God, there is a confusion of the orthodox concept of the Spirit's work in inspiration and illumination.

As has been indicated earlier neo-orthodoxy makes a sharp distinction between objective propositional truth and the subjective appropriations of it. For them the internal witness of the Spirit makes the Bible *become* at times the Word of God and at other times not the Word of God. This takes place only when God determines that it should for each man as it speaks to his personal situation.

Now it must be kept in mind that true orthodoxy does not deny the necessity of the Holy Spirit's work in the heart to make the truth of God understandable. That work of illumination, however, does not alter the objective character of the Word of God. Scripture is the Word of God whether it is made clear by the Spirit or not. The confusion of the work of the Holy Spirit in neo-orthodoxy is not the result of poor presentation or ignorance on their part. It is rather the end result of having rejected the fact that God has communicated truth about Himself.

Acceptance of radical higher criticism: Higher criticism is sometimes called historical criticism. It is a study which seeks to determine the authorship and dates of Biblical documents. The study delves into questions of canonicity, genuineness and credibility of books of the Bible.

Both higher and lower (textual) criticism are legitimate branches of study but both have been misused to cast aspersions upon the authority of Scripture. They have been so used by the liberal and neo-orthodox. Briefly summarizing the error of destructive radical criticism Young says: "This criticism presupposes that the investigator may subject the words of the Bible to his own unaided mind and may pass a judgment upon them."[25]

It is no secret that the neo-orthodox accept the Wellhausen higher critical theory; in fact their system rests solidly upon it.

Brunner spoke for others in the neo-orthodox camp when he bluntly said: "I myself am an adherent of a rather radical school of biblical criticism which, for example, does not accept the Gospel of John as a historical source and which finds legends in many parts of the synoptical gospels."[26]

This acceptance of destructive higher criticism places neo-orthodoxy squarely on the side of liberalism at this point and unquestionably against the traditional orthodox view and, most important of all, against the testimony of Christ and the Bible to its own inspiration.

Rejection of the historic orthodox doctrine: By virtue of the neo-orthodox acceptance of radical higher criticism there is a clear rejection of the historic church doctrine of the Scriptures. The higher critical view and the church doctrine are highly incompatible. The one is a clear repudiation of the other.

In spite of the denials of some that a church doctrine of Scripture exists there is abundant evidence to support that fact. Those who try to discredit belief in such a church doctrine usually do so by identifying verbal inspiration with the dictation theory of inspiration. That the two views are not synonymous has been clearly presented often.[27] To prove the existence of such a church doctrine it is not necessary to be able to appeal to some dogma of the church. Dogma and doctrine are not the same; for a doctrine may be held universally by the church without being immediately incorporated into the creeds of the church.

---

[25] Young, *op. cit.*, p. 243.

[26] Emil Brunner, *The Theology of Crisis* (New York: Charles Scribner's Sons, 1930), p. 41.

[27] See J. Gresham Machen, *Christianity and Liberalism* (Philadelphia: The Presbyterian Guardian, 1940), pp. 73-74.

There is abundant evidence that the church doctrine of Scripture incorporated belief in verbal plenary inspiration, inerrancy, and the authority of Scripture. Warfield summarizes the historic faith of the church regarding the Scriptures in the following words: "Nor do we need do more than remind ourselves that this attitude of entire trust in every word of the Scriptures has been characteristic of the people of God from the very foundation of the church. Christendom has always reposed upon the belief that the utterances of this book are properly oracles of God. The whole body of Christian literature bears witness to this fact. We may trace its stream to its source, and everywhere it is vocal with a living faith in the divine trustworthiness of the Scriptures of God in every one of their affirmations."[28]

It is indeed amazing that neo-orthodoxy would object to the historic orthodox position since it claims to be a return to orthodoxy. This it does, however, with vehemence. Barth rejects the doctrine vigorously while proposing to defend the hiddenness and freedom of God. To accept the orthodox view would be to bind the sovereign God to a finished revelation in Scripture according to Barth. One thing is crystal clear and that is that Barth's and his followers' position is not to be equated with the historic orthodox position.

Scripture a witness to Christ: Neo-orthodoxy accuses orthodoxy of putting the Bible in the place of Jesus Christ while the neo-orthodox are hailed as the ones who find revelation primarily in Christ. They want to be recognized as those who place Jesus Christ as the center and climax of God's revelation, with the Bible on the periphery pointing to Him, sometimes accurately and sometimes not so accurately.

Orthodoxy does not object to Christ as the revealer of God because the Bible proclaims Him to be just that. However, neo-orthodoxy errs in failing to view Christ as the completed revelation of God as He came at the first advent. It also fails to see that all that is known of Christ, as the revealer, is recorded in Scripture. If anything is to be known of Him as the revealer of God it must be learned from the words of Scripture.

---

[28] Benjamin Breckinridge Warfield, *The Inspiration and Authority of the Bible* (Philadelphia: The Presbyterian and Reformed Publishing Company, 1948), p. 107.

Inspiration not verbal: This is the crux of the issue and with such a view neo-orthodoxy blatantly contradicts the high view of Scripture held by Jesus Christ.

Barth uses the term "verbal" in his discussion of inspiration but he does not mean by it that the words of the Scripture are inspired. He means only that God *may* speak through the words. "Verbal inspiration does not mean: infallibility of the biblical word in its linguistic, historical, theological character as human word. Verbal inspiration does mean: the fallible and failing human word is now as such taken by God into his service, and to be accepted as such and heard notwithstanding its human fallibility."[29]

Again, Barth declares: "The inspiration of the Bible . . . does not lie before us as the Bible lies before us and as we read the Bible."[30] For Barth there is no verbal inspiration in the Bible. The Bible is God's Word only so far as God lets it be His Word, as He speaks through it.

Brunner agrees with Barth in his rejection of verbal inspiration. He says: "Only through a serious misunderstanding will genuine faith find satisfaction in the theory of verbal inspiration of the Bible."[31]

Reinhold Niebuhr's view is no different; for he too believes the Bible is marred by the same errors and inconsistencies that are found in anything produced by men.

Scripture not infallible: The net result of the rejection of verbal inspiration is a Bible that is fallible and untrustworthy. Evidence has already been presented showing the neo-orthodox rejection of the infallibility of Scripture. Rejection of propositional truth and thereby verbal inspiration inevitably results in a fallible Bible. Thus, the neo-orthodox view is that God speaks through the fallible Scriptures and makes them become, or at least point to, the Word of God. The neo-orthodox concept is that since God is not ashamed of the errors and contradictions in His Word why should we be.

Scripture not authoritative: Another unmistakable result in the neo-orthodox process of rejecting the Biblical view of Scripture is to reject all divine authority in the words of

[29] Karl Barth, *Church Dogmatics*, Vol. I, Part II: *The Doctrine of the Word of God*, trans. G. T. Thomson and Harold Knight (New York: Charles Scribner's Sons, 1956), p. 533.

[30] *Ibid.*, p. 523.

[31] Brunner, *The Theology of Crisis*, p. 19.

Scripture. Concerning the neo-orthodox view of the authority of Scripture Kantzer says: "Just at this point is to be found the 'Achilles' heel' of the neo-orthodox. By appealing from the written Scripture to a voice of the Spirit, they are in effect setting themselves over the Bible. They do not receive a teaching of the Bible because of the authority of the Bible. Rather they put the Bible through a sieve and receive from it only what comes through the sieve."[32]

That the above observation is a true picture of the neo-orthodox viewpoint will be demonstrated from the words of the neo-orthodox themselves. Brunner puts it bluntly: "The word of Scripture is not the final court of appeal, since Jesus Christ Himself alone is this ultimate authority; but even while we examine the doctrine of Scripture, we remain within Scripture, not, it is true, as an authority, but as the source of all that truth which possesses absolute authority."[33]

In criticizing Barth, Polman states: "Every transformation of God's Word into an infallible human word, and every conversion of the human words of the Bible into an infallible Word of God is a rebellion against the real wonder: that fallible human beings, in fallible human words, here utter God's Word."[34]

According to Barth the Bible as a book claims no authority for itself; it only wants to be a witness to revelation.

Criticizing the Reformation view of the authority of the Bible, Niebuhr says: "The Reformation insistence upon the authority of Scripture as against the authority of the church, bears within it the perils of a new idolatry. Its Biblicism became, in time, as dangerous to the freedom of the human mind in searching out causes and effects as the old religious authority. But rightly conceived Scriptural authority is meant merely to guard the truth of the gospel in which all truth is fulfilled and all corruptions of truth are negated. This authority is Scriptural in the sense that the culmination in Christ, of that *Heilsgeschichte* in which the whole human enterprise becomes fully conscious of its limits, and of the

---

[32] Kenneth Kantzer, "Neo-orthodoxy and the Inspiration of Scripture," *Bibliotheca Sacra,* CXVI (January, 1959), p. 27.

[33] Emil Brunner, *Dogmatics,* Vol. I: *Christian Doctrine of God* (Philadelphia: The Westminster Press, 1950), p. 47.

[34] A. D. R. Polman, *Barth* (Philadelphia: The Presbyterian and Reformed Publishing Co., 1960), p. 19.

divine answer to its problems. When the Bible becomes an authoritative compendium of social, economic, political and scientific knowledge it is used as a vehicle of the sinful sanctification of relative standards of knowledge and virtue which happen to be enshrined in a religious canon."[35]

From the above quotations it is obvious that there are differences among neo-orthodox thinkers concerning the degree of authority the Bible possesses. Even though the Bible is viewed differently by them they all concur on the fact that the fallible Bible is able to become God's Word and at that crisis moment, as it points to Christ, it is the authority for man's religious life. It is equally obvious that the historic orthodox view of the final authority of the very words of Scripture is completely rejected by the neo-orthodox.

The neo-orthodox view compared with Christ's view: Chapters Three and Four of this discussion have been occupied with a presentation of Christ's view of the inspiration and authority of Scripture. Therefore, it will not be necessary to reproduce the evidence cited there. It is only necessary to be reminded that He taught that the very words were inspired and that the whole of Scripture could not be broken or annulled (John 10:35). Thus it is paradoxically strange that the neo-orthodox would baldly reject the view of Scripture held by Christ, the very one they claim to exalt. If revelation centers in Him why may not He be trusted in His view of Scripture?

The neo-orthodox are on the horns of a dilemma when they seek to present a Jesus who is infallible in most areas but who held a faulty view of the Scriptures. When they say, as Brunner has, that to identify the words of the Bible with the Word of God is an error of most serious consequence and that recourse to a pronouncement of Scripture as a final court of appeal is impossible, they have struck at the very views of Christ who is God's revelation *in persona*.[36]

Though neo-orthodoxy claims to rest its ultimate authority in Christ it is obvious that it does not do so. Actually, the ultimate seat of authority in their view does not rest in the Bible, the church, the Holy Spirit, or Christ but in them-

---

[35] Reinhold Niebuhr, *Nature and Destiny of Man* (New York: Charles Scribner's Sons, 1943), II, 289.

[36] Paul King Jewett, "Emil Brunner's Doctrine of Scripture," *Inspiration and Interpretation*, ed. John F. Walvoord (Grand Rapids: Wm. B. Eerdmans Publishing Co., 1957), p. 232.

selves. Each individual Barthian becomes the subjective criterion for determining what is and what is not the Word of God.

Not only is there direct contrast between Christ's view and the neo-orthodox view regarding history and revelation then, but there is also very strong opposition by them to Christ's view of inspiration and authority. Kantzer has presented the issue plainly: "The issue may be presented even more decisively. Is Christ Lord or is He not Lord? If He is, then let us receive Him as Lord. And let us receive the view of Scripture which He believed and taught."[37] No one can rightly claim to exalt Christ and be His follower who seeks to set aside the Scripture.

---

[37] Kantzer, "Neo-orthodoxy and the Inspiration of Scripture," *Bibliotheca Sacra*, CXVI (January, 1959), 28.

CHAPTER VI

CONTEMPORARY DENIALS OF THE SAVIOUR'S TEACHING

PART II, NEO-LIBERALISM

DEFINITIONS

Old liberalism

Before any appreciable progress can be made some definitions are in order. The terms *old liberalism* and *new liberalism* have been referred to previously and their meanings must now be established.

The theological liberalism which prevailed prior to World War I has been variously defined. It is usually defined in terms of an attitude, a spirit or a method. For purposes of this study the clear definition given by Nels F. S. Ferré will suffice: "Liberalism was the attempt to give Christian content to the stream of man's general non-authoritative method based on reason, experience and history."[1] The obvious fact in this definition in relation to the present study of Bibliology is the liberal rejection of the infallibility and authority of Scripture for the subjective authority of man.

This is the brand of liberalism which met with great success in winning schools, churches and denominations to its presuppositions until World War I and the introduction of neo-orthodoxy into the theological scene.

Neo-liberalism

The repentant liberalism which recovered from the theologically devastating blows of the War and neo-orthodoxy

[1] Nels F. S. Ferré, "Contemporary Theology in the Light of 100 Years," *Theology Today*, XV (October, 1958), 369.

has come to be known as neo or new liberalism. Hordern defines it accurately as follows: "Neo-liberalism is the attempt to preserve the values of liberalism while reinterpreting them for a new age and new conditions."[2]

From this definition it is immediately apparent that the new liberalism is attempting to do two things. It is attempting to maintain the gains of the older liberalism and at the same time make those classic gains understandable for the present age and conditions. Because of this obvious and admitted fact the following discussion will deal primarily with the views of neo-liberals. There are still some who hold to the old liberalism; but for the most part all those who formerly ascribed to the old liberal school are now identified with neo-liberalism.

This similarity in essence between the old and new liberalism is not always admitted by neo-liberals. Some of them claim to occupy a place so different from the early liberals that they resent being identified with them. This resentment must be rejected, however, because the differences are superficial and mere surface differences since the subjective view of authority continues to underlie both. New liberalism is nothing more than old liberalism in new garments.

The Christ of Neo-liberalism

What view is being held regarding Christ by these "converted liberals"? The answer to this question will help in the understanding of their view of Scripture and explain the reason for their rejection of Christ's view.

Background for the view

From the rise of classic liberalism in Schleiermacher to the time of its decline in Karl Barth there was a tendency to do away with any intermediaries between God and man. Man was viewed as being so good and God so present in the world that the Jesus of the Gospels was unnecessary for most liberals. It is indeed very difficult to find the exact role of Jesus in liberal theology because liberals are not agreed among themselves as to His place in history. Some early liberals

---

[2] William Hordern, *A Layman's Guide to Protestant Theology* (New York: The Macmillan Company, 1955), p. 100.

solved the problems which they found in this doctrine by concluding that the Jesus portrayed in the New Testament never really existed. Listen to the words of Albert Schweitzer: "The Jesus of Nazareth who came forward publicly as the Messiah, who preached the ethics of the kingdom of God, who founded the Kingdom of Heaven upon earth, and died to give his work its final consecration, never had any existence."[3] Schweitzer, like others, believed that Paul and the other New Testament writers did not present the Jesus of history but rather the Jesus of their making.

This was the result of the liberal quest behind and beyond the Gospels for the Jesus of history who was to be distinguished from the Christ of faith. The Jesus which this search invented may be called the "liberal Jesus." Though the liberals viewed Him as a good man conscious of God as no other man was He was barely distinguishable from the rest of the human race. Liberals have never had nor do they now have a clear concept of His deity or of His humanity. They have been satisfied to deny His true deity and to deride the orthodox concept of His humanity.

It was neo-orthodoxy that invaded and became victorious over the old liberal view of Christ. Neo-orthodoxy refused to accept the "liberal Jesus." The Jesus which the liberals invented was too little like God and too much like man for the neo-orthodox. Thus, liberalism's doctrine of Christ was sorely challenged and made bereft; and as a result a "new" doctrine of Christ has been developed by the contemporary liberals.

Neo-liberal reinterpretation

Neo-liberals began their reinterpretation of the doctrine of Christ by building upon the work of old liberalism in the discovery of the Jesus of history. They have given grateful recognition to the service which liberalism had rendered in discovering behind the Gospels the real Jesus of history. In accepting the old liberal foundations the new liberalism seeks to avoid the dilemma which its forefathers faced of either being forced to admit that the Gospel records are unreliable

---

[3] Albert Schweitzer, *The Quest of the Historical Jesus* (New York: The Macmillan Company, 1950), p. 398.

or that Jesus was capable of error and therefore very unliberal in His theology.

Thus, a new portrait of Jesus is being painted today, a portrait different from that which the liberals or the reformers produced and certainly different from the Biblical idea of an all-knowing God becoming man.

The method by which neo-liberals are developing this completely "new" portrait of Jesus is through the re-evaluation of His incarnation, deity, death and resurrection. Accepting the findings of destructive higher criticism which reconstructs and reclassifies the origin, dates, sources and authorship of Biblical books neo-liberalism proceeds to restate its unbelief in believable language. Only after the critic has mutilated the text in the name of scholarship can the sayings of Christ really be ascribed to Him. He is said to have used the Old Testament with His own kind of criticism. In fact, some claim that Jesus said nothing about the factual accuracy of Scripture.[4] This of course is only said after the teachings of the Saviour have gone through the liberal mincing machine.

Contemporary liberalism rejects the testimony of the Bible and the historic creeds of the church regarding the person and work of Christ. Speaking of the ancient Creed of Chalcedon which was an attempt to establish the perfect deity and humanity of Christ, Van Dusen says: ". . . its teminology sounds like distilled nonsense. . . . It is as though the Fathers were determined to affirm their certainties at whatever humiliation to reason."[5] A distinction is also made in neo-liberal theology between the facts of history and the interpretation of those facts. They often seek to discover the fact apart from the faith of the Christian community and this relates particularly to the resurrection of Christ.

Oxnam admits that to believe in the doctrine of the incarnation requires a leap of faith. He finds it difficult to believe in the virgin birth because Jesus never mentioned it;

---

[4] Daniel B. Stevick, *Beyond Fundamentalism* (Richmond: John Knox Press, 1964), pp. 87-89.

[5] David E. Roberts and Henry Pitney Van Dusen (eds.), *Liberal Theology* (New York: Charles Scribner's Sons, 1942), p. 208.

neither did James, Peter or John. For him it is not necessary to believe in the virgin birth to affirm belief in the deity of Christ.[6]

DeWolf doubts the virgin birth of Christ because it is apparent that the neighbors in Nazareth knew nothing about it.[7] The necessity of the virgin birth is questioned since it is mentioned in only a few of the Biblical records. Obviously, if belief in the incarnation involves a leap of faith and belief in the virgin birth requires a still greater leap, there is no need to investigate further into the Biblical presentation of His deity. The weak and insipid explanation of the Saviour's deity as explained by DeWolf summarizes the neo-liberal viewpoint. "Jesus, in his controlling center of motivation and purpose, not only stands closer to God than does any other man; he is capable of being fully understood only by God, and God can be properly known only by those who are enabled to do so by Jesus."[8]

It is certain that with the above concepts regarding the person of Christ and with an acceptance of destructive higher criticism the contemporary liberal view of Scripture will fall far short of that held by Christ and presented by the human writers of Scripture.

The Revelation of God in Scripture

There are similarities in the neo-orthodox and contemporary liberal views of special revelation, or revelation in the Bible, and therefore it will not be necessary to repeat here what has already been presented as the neo-orthodox concept. Temple boldly states the contemporary liberal view of revelation in Scripture: "There is no such thing as revealed truth. . . . There are truths of revelation, that is to say, propositions which express the results of correct thinking concerning revelation; but they are not themselves directly revealed."[9]

---

[6] G. Bromley Oxnam, *A Testament of Faith* (Cambridge, Massachusetts: Little, Brown & Co., 1958), p. 32.

[7] L. Harold DeWolf, *The Case for Theology in Liberal Perspective* (Philadelphia: The Westminster Press, 1959), p. 61.

[8] *Ibid.*, p. 63.

[9] William Temple, *Nature, Man and God* (London: The Macmillan Company, 1954), p. 317.

Let us observe the path which led from the Biblical and historical view that the Bible was the deposit of revealed truths, the very recorded utterances of God, to the above denunciation of that conviction.

Historical antecedents to the neo-liberal view

It was not until the Middle Ages that church tradition was viewed as that which authenticated and interpreted Scripture. Even this did not alter the prevailing view of the nature of Scripture. It merely meant that the pronouncements of the church were being placed on an equally high level with Scripture. This Roman concept replaced the ministry of the Spirit with the ministry of the church. The task of the Reformers was to disentangle Scripture from the traditions of the church. From the seventeenth century to the present hour there has been a consistent and constant attack upon the view of Scripture held by the early church and the Reformers.

The original concepts of special revelation in the Bible such as its verbal character, its relation to Israel and its finality in written form have been under severe attack.

These concepts were gradually modified and watered down and finally abandoned by many. Rationalism and mysticism with their subjectivism and acceptance of higher criticism eliminated belief in special revelation almost entirely from the theological spectrum.

Contemporary liberalism faces a dilemma indeed. It stands before the older orthodox view which recognized the objective character of revelation in the Bible and was thus based on verbal inspiration and inerrancy. This view is rejected in light of the scientific discoveries of the higher critical view. After having accepted the findings of higher criticism liberalism has again found itself sorely bereft by neo-orthodoxy which has proven the liberal position untenable by its rejection of any propositional revelation.

Packer has stated the resultant contemporary liberal problem well: "The problem, therefore, as modern theology conceives it, is this: how can the concept of divine revelation through the Bible be reintroduced without reverting to the old, 'unscientific' equation of the Bible with the Word of

God?"[10] The same writer adds a further word of explanation of the problem: "The problem is, how to enthrone the Bible once more as judge of the errors of man while leaving man enthroned as judge of the errors of the Bible; how to commend the Bible as a true witness while continuing to charge it with falsehood."[11]

Scripture a witness to revelation

Modern theology almost unanimously regards Scripture as a human response and witness to revelation but not revelation itself. It was noted in the previous chapter that this was true of the neo-orthodox concept of Scripture. Here it will be observed that this idea is held with fervor among the neo-liberal branch of contemporary theology. Revelation is never to be identified with any human words recorded in Scripture. The neo-liberal concept is that revelation must be received before it becomes actual and real revelation. Communication is not complete until what has been given is received. While they are willing to call the Bible the Word of God this is not intended in any way to convey the idea that the Bible is the pure Word of God.

Walter Marshall Horton, an outstanding neo-liberal, has put it bluntly: "There are some ancient misunderstandings about revelation which do not seriously threaten us at present, after the debates of the last half-century. We are not likely again to identify God's eternal Word with the Book which contains the record of its revealing, or to insist that everything in that Book is infallibly correct and verbally inspired."[12]

There are many areas of agreement and some areas of disagreement between the neo-orthodox and the neo-liberal view of Scripture. Perhaps the basic difference between the two views lies in the fact that neo-liberalism admits inspiration for parts of the Bible even though it contains a mixture of truth and error. Neo-orthodoxy rejects any objective truth in the Bible and states that the Bible is only the record of past revelatory events and contains no revelation *per se*.

---

[10] James I. Packer, "Contemporary Views of Revelation," *Revelation and the Bible*, ed. Carl F. H. Henry (Grand Rapids: Baker Book House, 1958), p. 94.

[11] *Ibid.*

[12] Walter Marshall Horton, "Revelation," *Revelation*, ed. John Baillie and Hugh Martin (London: Faber & Faber Limited, 1937), p. 264.

Nels F. S. Ferre shows the neo-liberal agreement with and divergence from the neo-orthodox view of revelation in the following two statements. Divergence is seen when he says: "The Bible is an objective strand of history reporting man's response to God's Christ-deed, his sending of the Holy Spirit, and his founding of the Church."[13] The agreement which neo-liberalism has with neo-orthodoxy in this area is seen in this statement about the original faith-witnesses: "Because they responded as finite human beings, touched with sin, to the holy facts of God's saving presence and mighty acts, the biblical record shows us the absolute truth but not absolutely."[14] What this really amounts to is the neo-liberal attempt to pawn off one brand of subjectivism for another and in the process all real objectivity is removed from the record. The fallacy of this subjective approach is easily seen. If the Bible is no more than a human witness to revelation what guarantee do we have that our ideas about it are true ideas since we are sinners?

Scripture not a completed revelation

Neo-liberals consider belief in the Bible as a collection of theological doctrines an obstacle to faith. Their story is almost always the same. Some express their unbelief more cleverly and cautiously than others but it is there nevertheless. Otto A. Piper spoke for contemporary liberalism when he admitted that ". . . the greatest obstacle to my understanding of the Bible—and I suppose many people experience the same difficulty—was my belief that the Bible was a collection of theological doctrines plus a record of historical events."[15]

The Bible is viewed by the liberal as a norm, not a final norm, but one which can be maneuvered so as to be made to agree with contemporary learning and scientific discovery. Thus, it is a flexible and adaptable norm.

Rejection of Scripture as the final and completed revelation of God is also seen in the words of the late G. Bromley Oxnam. In his discussion of the possibility of revealed truth,

---

[13] Nels F. S. Ferré, *Where Do We Go from Here in Theology?* (Pierce & Washabaught, Winter, 1955-56), pp. 10-11.

[14] *Ibid.*, p. 11.

[15] Otto A. Piper, "The Theme of the Bible," *The Christian Century*, LXIII (March, 1946), 334.

he acknowledges the fact that God has revealed Himself *progressively* through the centuries to limited human beings. He writes: "The revelation was conditioned by their ability to understand, and their reports bear evidence of the limitations that current events, and current practice evoke. Take the cosmology accepted by the Old Testament writers, for instance; or the belief in demons; or Paul's attitude toward women. To hold that Paul's advice on women is truth revealed by God and binding upon all is as sorry as to hold that God commanded the Jews to commit atrocities on their enemies in war. Nonetheless truth is revealed."[16]

Now, it is true that God did not reveal everything about Himself at one time and to one individual. However, this in no way implies that what He revealed earlier is less true than what He revealed later. Progressive revelation does not mean progressive inspiration. Such a view of Scripture is not only diametrically opposed to the historic orthodox position but is also at odds with the Bible's witness to itself and the witness of Jesus Christ to Scripture.

THE INSPIRATION OF THE SCRIPTURES

It is a logical fact that one's view of revelation sets boundaries to his view of inspiration. This is illustrated clearly in both neo-orthodoxy and neo-liberalism. Both schools of thought hold common ground in the rejection of the Saviour's view of the revelation and inspiration of Scripture. The basic presuppositions of both systems have been derived from the subjective philosophy of Schleiermacher. However differently they may state their viewpoints they join in rejecting any identification of God's truth with the written record in Scripture.

The agreement is not complete, however, and this fact will become obvious in the discussion to follow. The Biblical emphasis of neo-orthodoxy has driven contemporary liberalism to a higher appreciation of the Bible and this is sometimes styled a return to Biblical theology. This supposed return will now be studied before the doctrine of inspiration is pursued.

---

[16] Oxnam, *op. cit.*, p. 135.

Neo-liberal return to a "Biblical theology"

It is a commonly accepted fact that classic liberalism had little appreciation for the Bible. Liberal theologians of the eighteenth century did not even take the Bible seriously. They believed that revealed religion was false and untrustworthy. As far as they were concerned the records were completely unreliable. The neo-orthodox emphasis upon the Bible drove liberalism to reevaluate the value of Scripture.[17]

It must not be supposed that this so-called return to Biblical theology has been a return on the part of liberals to the claims of historic Christianity and of the Bible itself to its authority. Those who claim to proclaim a Biblical theology and at the same time reject the theological propositions of the Bible are caught on the horns of a dilemma. They now desire to view the Bible from the inside out, rather than from the outside in. Packer shows the neo-liberal dilemma when he evaluates this proposal: "They can hardly be unaware that, if they were consistent in reading the Bible 'from within' and receiving what its authors were concerned to teach, they would be led to the doctrine of Scripture which we have expounded; for that doctrine is integral to the biblical faith."[18]

Actually the "return" to "Biblical theology" is not a return at all except to some of the terminology of Biblicism. "The new Liberals are anxious to be biblical in their beliefs, and condemn old Liberalism as heretical; but they are held back from a consistently biblical outlook by the legacy of rationalistic criticism which they have inherited. . . . The self-contradictory character of liberal Christianity has never become more evident than here. . . . The truth is that 'Biblical Theology' wants to have it both ways. . . . It wants to be able to commend itself to the world as scientific, because it holds to the unorthodox views of nineteenth century critics, and to the Church as Christian, because it deals with 'the biblical point of view.' "[19]

---

[17] Robert P. Lightner, *Neo-Liberalism* (Chicago: Regular Baptist Press, 1959), p. 40.

[18] J. I. Packer, *"Fundamentalism" and the Word of God* (Grand Rapids: Wm. B. Eerdmans Publishing Co., 1960), p. 152.

[19] *Ibid.*, pp. 154-56.

The most basic reason for rejecting the return to "Biblical theology" is because of the neo-liberal acceptance of destructive higher criticism.

Neo-liberal acceptance of destructive higher criticism

This too is an accepted fact and need not be labored here. A few quotations will suffice to establish the fact. The neo-liberal acceptance of destructive higher criticism is the result of its desire to preserve the "abiding values" of old liberalism. This is one of the essential areas of agreement which neo-liberalism has with old liberalism.

DeWolf argues that destructive higher criticism should be retained by liberalism. He says: "The insistence of some conservative Christians on a Biblical literalism that is rationally indefensible and an appeal based on the 'proofs' of prophecy and miracles, in defiance of the natural sciences and the new historical understanding of Biblical times, needlessly drives from the Christian faith intelligent young people who will not blind themselves to scientific and historical evidences."[20]

Liberals do not object to the recent interest in the Bible so long as there is not a return to what they call the uncritical and anti-scientific viewpoint of conservatism. The higher critical view is regarded as subject to continual review and correction but never with the anticipation of surrender to the orthodox position. Liberals firmly believe higher criticism rests on a solid foundation.[21]

Along with this whole-hearted acceptance of higher criticism goes the rejection of verbal plenary inspiration and inerrancy.

Neo-liberal denial of verbal inspiration

This denial has been stated boldly by some and less boldly by others. Nevertheless it is the prevailing attitude of neo-liberals to reject the traditional orthodox view of the verbal plenary inspiration of Scripture.

---

[20] DeWolf, *op. cit.*, p. 43.
[21] Stevick, *op. cit.*, p. 97.

Before presenting the proof for this denial it will be well to summarize the confusion prevalent today over certain terms and some of the false charges made against the time-honored doctrine of verbal plenary inspiration.

The historic Protestant understanding of revelation has been that it relates to the act of God whereby He communicated knowledge of Himself and His will to men. Inspiration has been understood to refer to the God-breathed record of that revelation. Illumination relates to the divine enablement to understand the recorded revelation.

Neo-liberals, and they are not alone in this, use these terms interchangeably and by so doing do them a great injustice. John Baillie, for example, confuses inspiration with enlightenment. Concerning inspiration he says: "Its meaning and scope have often been misconceived through its being applied primarily to the prophets and apostolic witness, and withal their written witness, to the revelation rather than to the illumination of the prophetic and apostolic mind which is an integral part of the revelation to which such witness is borne."[22] Baillie puts revelation and inspiration on different levels. He further says: "In what is given of God there can be no imperfection of any kind, but there is always imperfection in what we may be allowed to call the 'receiving apparatus.' "[23]

Thus it is evident that intentionally or unintentionally neo-liberalism approaches the Scriptures, and the conservative view of them, with a confusion of the doctrines involved. Contemporary liberal writers frequently identify verbal plenary inspiration with dictation and mechanical writing. They often link the doctrines of inerrancy with what they choose to call "bare literalism" by which they mean that the adherents believe every word must be interpreted literally, even those which are obviously figures of speech.

These charges are not true and will not stand the searchlights of conservative scholarship. With all the available information on the conservative position one can only assume that these charges are made because the errors they present are easier to refute than the actual conservative position.

---

[22] John Baillie, *The Idea of Revelation in Recent Thought* (New York: Columbia University Press, 1956), p. 66.

[23] *Ibid.*, p. 34.

The denial of the historic orthodox doctrine of verbal plenary inspiration and inerrancy[24] is universal among neo-liberals. Speaking of the Bible, DeWolf plainly says, "In it are to be found the erring words of men as well as the authoritative word of God."[25] Along the same line the same writer continues: "The reader who would hear the true word of God in the reading of the Bible must be prepared to discriminate between the word of God and the words of men."[26]

It is obvious from these two quotations that DeWolf's deciding factor of where the Bible is the Word of God and where it is the word of man is the individual reader. As an attempt to evade the complete subjectivity of such an approach DeWolf lists four criteria which must be taken into consideration before the determination can be made. These criteria are the literary context, historical context, Christian context and total perspective.[27] The attempt is unsuccessful and the pure subjectivity is not removed. Another very recent publication by one who claims to have gone beyond fundamentalism reveals the extent of the author's journey. His conviction is that ". . . . even to make the affirmation of biblical inerrancy is philosophically perilous."[28] He boldly asserts: "It is not the case that the Bible is from end to end 'the documented revelation of God.' "[29] This author recognizes the subjective nature of his charges and of his own view and his attempt to excuse it is just so much more subjectivism.

This method of picking and choosing distinguishes neo-liberalism from neo-orthodoxy. Neo-orthodoxy rejects any propositional record of truth in the words of the Bible. They do not even pick and choose.

The question has often been asked, but the answer has never been fully accepted by either neo-orthodoxy or neo-liberalism: If the Bible is only infallible and inspired in selected parts, where is its authority?

---

[24] See Packer, *"Fundamentalism" and the Word of God*, p. 79 where he explains the use of the word *dictation* in the sixteenth and seventeenth centuries. Also, see pp. 94-101 for a clear discussion of the meaning of *infallible* and *inerrant* and the historic orthodox position on them.

[25] DeWolf, *op. cit.*, p. 47.

[26] *Ibid.*, p. 48.

[27] *Ibid.*, pp. 49-55.

[28] Stevick, *op. cit.*, p. 82.

[29] *Ibid.*, p. 106.

In his book *A Layman's Guide to Protestant Theology* Hordern deals with what he calls "modern orthodoxy." Actually, there is no recognizable difference between modern orthodoxy and neo-liberalism and Hordern admits the proximity between them. Concerning the view of the Bible held by this form of neo-liberalism he says: "The doctrine of the verbal inspiration of the Bible is viewed by modern orthodoxy as a deviation from the traditional position of orthodoxy. Though modern orthodoxy welcomes the liberal concern to re-express the ancient truths in terms that the modern world can comprehend, it feels that liberals often lost the truth along with the ancient forms of expression."[30]

Thus without need of further proof it can be seen that neo-liberalism rejects the doctrine of verbal plenary inspiration and substitutes in its place a view of Scripture which places man in the authoritative position of determining which parts are and which are not the Word of God. The reason for this approach is twofold. First of all, it results from the high view of man which the liberal holds, and secondly neo-liberalism is thus seeking to preserve what it terms the humanity in the Bible. In other words neo-liberalism does not regard the Holy Spirit, if Holy Spirit there be, capable of preserving the human writers from all error and omission in the production of Scripture.

Neo-liberal denial of the infallibility of Scripture

Such a watered-down view of Scripture naturally leads to a denial of the infallibility of Scripture. This denial will be briefly presented.

The word "infallible" refers to the quality of never deceiving or misleading, and therefore means that the subject to which it is applied is completely trustworthy and reliable. It was just such a conviction of Scripture which Christ expressed when He said "scripture cannot be broken" (John 10:35) and ". . . Till heaven and earth pass, one jot or one tittle shall in no wise pass from the law till all be fulfilled" (Matt. 5:18).

Neo-liberalism blatantly contradicts, therefore, not only the historic view of the church on this matter but also the head of the church, Jesus Christ.

[30] Hordern, *op. cit.*, p. 186.

Baillie writes: "Nothing could be more artificial than to suppose that these writers were endowed with infallibility in all that they had in mind to say, while the Holy Spirit left them to their own devices as to how they should say it."[31]

After rejecting the Roman Catholic doctrine of an infallible interpreter in the pope, DeWolf declares, "Besides, the Bible itself is by no means infallible."[32] The same writer goes on to attempt to show that the doctrine of the infallibility of Scripture is untenable because of such things as the teaching of Revelation 7:13-17 compared with Ecclesiastes 9:2-5.[33] He concludes by saying, "The doctrine of infallibility is quite impossible in practice, for one cannot put into living faith flatly contrary teachings."[34]

Modern attempts are being made to make a sharp distinction between the view of Biblical infallibility held by the early church and the Reformers and that held by contemporary conservatism especially as it is represented in fundamentalism.[35] The distinction is usually made by ascribing undue allegoricalism to the ancient view and unfounded literalism to the contemporary view. Finlayson put the conservative position succinctly: "The inspiration which we claim for the Scripture is the inspiration which the Scriptures claim for themselves, which the Apostolic Church claimed for them, and what the Reformed Church understood by the Word of God written.[36]

THE AUTHORITY OF THE SCRIPTURES

It is not the purpose of this section to treat the understanding of authority in general in neo-liberalism but only to deal with the authority of the Bible. The view of the authority of Scripture in neo-liberalism is self-evident from the above presentations of its view of revelation and inspira-

---

[31] Baillie, *op. cit.*, p. 115.

[32] DeWolf, *op. cit.*, p. 47.

[33] *Ibid.*, p. 56.

[34] *Ibid.*

[35] See J. K. S. Reid, *The Authority of Scripture* (New York: Harper and Brothers Publishers, n.d.), pp. 19-28 and A. G. Hebert, *The Authority of the Old Testament* (London: Faber & Faber, 1947), p. 98.

[36] R. A. Finlayson, "Contemporary Ideas of Inspiration," *Revelation and the Bible*, ed. Carl F. H. Henry (Grand Rapids: Baker Book House, 1958), p. 233.

tion. However, the salient features of the neo-liberal concept will be presented.

Authority not equal throughout the Bible

As has been noted earlier neo-liberalism does not agree with neo-orthodoxy in denying authority to *all* of the Bible. Rather it seeks to find authority in selected parts. DeWolf makes this fact clear. He writes of moderate liberalism or neo-liberalism: "They accept wholeheartedly the use of textual and historical criticism in the study of the Bible, while taking the Bible seriously as a great storehouse of divinely inspired wisdom. Some parts of the Bible they regard as much more valuable and authoritative than others. Supremely important are the accounts of Jesus and his teachings."[37]

Voicing the same opinion Ferré says: "To place everything on one level, stories of rape and the Sermon on the Mount, songs of hate and the Cross of Christ, is to be guilty of what Gerald Kennedy calls, I repeat, 'the crime of the levelers.' "[38]

H. H. Rowley, the famous Old Testament critic, asserts the very same pick-and-choose attitude. He writes: "The authority of Scripture is the authority of God. This does not mean that every statement of the Bible is to be unquestioningly accepted as the utterance of God, since that would be to ignore the human elements that went into its making. . . . We but dishonor God when we hold him responsible for every statement in the Bible."[39]

This section may be concluded with the piercing words of Temple. As to the Bible he said, ". . . the message is . . . so inextricably human and divine in one, that no single sentence can be quoted as having the authority of an authentic utterance of the All-Holy God."[40]

---

[37] L. Harold DeWolf, *Present Trends in Christian Thought* (New York: Association Press, 1960), p. 17.

[38] Nels F. S. Ferré, *Searchlights on Contemporary Theology* (New York: Harper & Brothers, 1961), p. 171.

[39] H. H. Rowley, "Authority and Scripture: I," *The Christian Century*, LXXVIII (March 1, 1961), 263.

[40] Temple, *op. cit.*, p. 350.

Authority not in words of the Bible

This concept is held in varying degrees by neo-liberals and to the extent in which authority is not associated with the words there is agreement with neo-orthodoxy. DeWolf expresses his opinion as follows: "There is high authority to be found in the Scripture, but this authority is not a general uniform authority of the words 'from cover to cover.' The authority of the word of God resides precisely in those teachings through which God speaks now to the living faith of the reader."[41]

Since it has already been established that neo-liberalism does not accept the doctrine of verbal inspiration it logically follows that it would reject any divine authority in words of the Bible, at least in all of the words. This concluding statement by Dillenberger and Welch exposes the neo-liberal view at this point and also reveals its own inherent problems: "While the Bible cannot be accepted as *absolute* authority (this belongs only to God), it does have *relative* authority over the preaching of the church and the individual experience. It provides the norm by which both personal experience and the doctrines of the church are to be judged."[42]

Authority in Christ

If the authority of Scripture is not to be universally applied to all the Bible and if it does not reside in the words of the Bible then where does it rest? The usual stock reply to such a question by the neo-liberals is that the authority of Scripture resides in the authority of Christ.

Ferré in his *Know Your Faith* presents and rejects three candidates for authority. These he lists as experience, the Bible and the church.[43] He rejects these including the Bible and states: "The upshot of the evaluation of the three contending positions—experience, the Bible, and the church—is as follows: Christ alone is the authority of the Christian

---

[41] DeWolf, *The Case for Theology in Liberal Perspective*, p. 56.

[42] John Dillenberger and Claude Welch, *Protestant Christianity Interpreted Through Its Development* (New York: Charles Scribner's Sons, 1954), p. 276.

[43] Nels F. S. Ferré, *Know Your Faith* (New York: Harper & Brothers Publishers, 1959), pp. 18-28.

faith."[44] Ferré concludes by explaining what he means by Christ as the sole authority: "Thus again we have as authority not the Christ of the Bible nor in the Bible, but the Christ who has come to us through the Bible and still can come to us through the Bible."[45] The same writer expresses the same conviction elsewhere: "No, we need a criterion, and the only criterion for the Bible is Christ."[46]

Reid may be cited as illustrative of the neo-liberal attempt to reject the authority of Scripture and at the same time to hold on to Christ as authoritative. His theological double-talk is evident as he writes: "If the authority of the Bible be located, not in the words of Holy Scripture, but rather in the Word itself, if it be located not in the printed page, but in Him to whom the printed page bears witness, Jesus Christ Himself the Word incarnate, crucified, risen, and regnant, in the transmitted message rather than in the transmitted letter, it will be possible to accommodate the results of criticisms of the words, and yet to credit the Bible with all the authority of Him to whom it testifies."[47]

Beegle's book, *The Inspiration of Scripture,* is a futile attempt to reject the inerrancy and infallibility of Scripture and at the same time to claim to hold Christ's view of the Scriptures. After rejecting Christ's words in Matthew 5:17, 18 and John 10:34, 35 as relating to the total inerrancy of Scripture he states: "It is time that all Christians make certain that their foundation is in Christ and his view of Scripture."[48]

Authority that is subjective

Thus, it has been demonstrated that in one way or another or to one degree or another neo-liberalism presents a purely subjective approach to the authority of Scripture. Authority is taken away from the Bible and placed into the hands of the reader. Even when they speak of Christ as authority neo-liberals must pick and choose because they reject what this authoritative Christ said about the authority of

[44] *Ibid.*, p. 29.
[45] *Ibid.*, p. 24.
[46] Ferré, *Searchlights on Contemporary Theology*, p. 171.
[47] Reid, *op. cit.*, p. 28.
[48] Dewey M. Beegle, *The Inspiration of Scripture* (Philadelphia: The Westminster Press, 1963), p. 188.

Scripture. All the efforts on the part of liberals to escape this subjectivism only produces more of it.

Bernard Ramm has stated clearly three reasons why the kind of authority presented by the liberals is defective: "(1) A revelation with no truth-content is a pseudo-revelation and therefore possesses no authority. . . . (2) A revelation made coterminous with religious experience destroys the notion of revelation, making it too extensive; and with the destruction of the principle of revelation the principle of authority in religion is destroyed. . . . (3) In view of the previous remarks it may now be urged that a revelation defined so subjectively cannot avoid a subjectivism which puts an end to revelation and authority."[49]

The defective nature of neo-liberal doctrine of the authority of Scripture evidences itself most clearly as it is compared with the teaching of the Saviour on the subject.

The Neo-Liberal View Compared with Christ's View

Without repeating what has already been presented in Chapters Two, Three and Four as the view of Christ regarding Scripture, it will be advantageous to point out a few of the crucial areas of divergence in the neo-liberal doctrine of Scripture from the views of Christ.

Christ taught that men wrote the Scripture; yet this human element in the Scriptures in no way militated against His firm conviction that what was written was precisely what God wanted written. The contemporary liberal viewpoint seems to be that if it be admitted that men wrote the Bible it must also be admitted that the Bible is fallible because men are fallible. In contradistinction to this false proposition, Christ taught that men did write the Scriptures, and yet they were so controlled by the Spirit that what they wrote was the infallible Word of God.

As was presented in Chapter Three He also taught the verbal inspiration of Scripture in several ways, particularly by His reference to the fulfillment of every "jot" and "tittle." This the liberal candidly denies.

Chapter Four presented the teaching of Christ regarding His own authority and the authority of Scripture. Con-

---

[49] Bernard Ramm, *The Pattern of Authority* (Grand Rapids: Wm. B. Eerdmans Publishing Co., 1957), pp. 78-81.

temporary liberalism wants to place the authority of Christ above the authority of Scripture. This is without question contrary to Christ's own teaching. He did stress His own authority many times but He also subjected His authority to the authority of Scripture (Matt. 4:4; John 10:34-35).

Reid attempts to overcome the problem which neo-liberalism faces in its divergence from the teaching of Christ by placing what Christ said regarding the Old Testament into two classifications. "There is a class of sayings (or actions) in which He improves upon what is written in the Scriptures He knew, and another where He endorses what is there."[50] Such a forced dissecting of the words of Christ will not stand under a thorough and exhaustive study of Christ's teaching and has been refuted in chapter two. Furthermore, the hypocrisy of turning to a proof text to substantiate a liberal concept is hardly in keeping with the liberal criticism of those who use such a method.

Packer silences the entire liberal approach to Scripture and its deviation from the view of Christ. He writes: "As we saw, Christ taught the principle of biblical authority quite unambiguously. Any sort of subjectivism, therefore, involves rejecting His authority as a teacher at this point. . . . Liberalism declares in effect that Christ was wrong, and labors to correct Him. But by what right may a disciple thus patronize his Master? 'Why call ye me, Lord, Lord, and do not the things which I say?' "[51]

Similarly, Gordon Clark in his critique of the views of inspiration presented in the December 24, 1962 issue of *The Presbyterian Outlook* under the general title "Do We Need an Infallible Bible?" exposes the neo-liberal and neo-orthodox attempt to hold to the authority of Christ and to reject the authority and infallibility of the Scriptures which He so staunchly proclaimed.[52]

---

[50] Reid, *op. cit.*, pp. 260-61.

[51] Packer, *"Fundamentalism" and the Word of God*, pp. 160-61.

[52] Gordon H. Clark, "Holy Scripture," *Bulletin of the Evangelical Theological Society*, VI (Winter, 1963), 3-7.

CHAPTER VII

CONTEMPORARY DEVIATIONS FROM THE SAVIOUR'S TEACHING

The confusing theological world has been further confused by the rise of a new phenomenon from within the evangelical camp. This new expression has enough agreements with orthodoxy to be called evangelical and enough differences to be called "neo" or "new." The leaders of the movement want to make certain that they are not in agreement with liberalism or neo-orthodoxy but they are in disagreement with fundamentalism, at least what they wish to call obscurantist elements in fundamentalism. The followers of this new expression of evangelicalism are referred to by others and sometimes self-styled as "repentant fundamentalists," "neo-evangelicals" or "new evangelicals," and sometimes simply "evangelicals." The name is not the important thing. What is more important is the theological viewpoints held by those in the movement. For our consideration it will be necessary to compare Christ's view of Scripture with those who quite obviously are dissatisfied with areas of the church doctrine of Scripture which doctrine has been embraced by and large by fundamentalism. We are not concerned here with the agreements or the disagreements which the new evangelicalism has with any other theological position, be it conservative or nonconservative. We are only concerned with the conformity or lack of conformity which neo-evangelicalism has with the Saviour's view of Scripture.[1]

---

[1] See the author's *Neo-Evangelicalism* (Chicago, Illinois: Regular Baptist Press, 1965). Part II chapter 1.

Background

The exact beginning date for the new evangelical emphasis is somewhat difficult to determine. The phrase *the new evangelicalism* was coined in an address at a convocation at Fuller Theological Seminary in 1948.[2] The attitude began earlier than this, but after the actual introduction of the term the dissatisfaction with fundamentalism became vocal. The approach is actually an outgrowth of fundamentalism and its controversy with liberalism. Its leaders are former fundaamentalists who became dissatisfied with fundamentalism.

Carl F. H. Henry, a respected conservative theologian, speaks as one representing the right of center position in neo-evangelicalism. His dissatisfactions with fundamentalism therefore should not be considered an unfair representation. These he lists as: displaced doctrinal responsibilities, a corrective theological emphasis, lack of theological and historical perspectives, tendency toward anti-denominationalism, emphasis upon premillennial dispensationalism and a shifted emphasis.[3]

Definition

A concise definition is difficult to state since many variations exist within the movement. Neo-evangelicalism represents those differing from neo-orthodoxy, liberalism and fundamentalism in certain attitudes and emphases yet showing appreciation for and/or affinity to these three. It is characterized by a respect for non-conservatism and a desire to be respected by it. Also, it is characterized by a strong emphasis upon the social application of the gospel.

Perhaps a definitive statement by one of the founding fathers will clarify the meaning: "The new evangelicalism breaks with . . . three movements. The new evangelicalism breaks first with neo-orthodoxy because it declares that it accepts the authority of the Bible. . . . He (the new evangelical) breaks with the modernist, however, in reference to his embrace of the full orthodox system of doctrine against that

---

[2] Harold John Ockenga, "The New Evangelicalism," *The Park Street Spire* (February, 1958), p. 7.

[3] Carl F. H. Henry, *Evangelical Responsibility in Contemporary Theology* (Grand Rapids: Wm. B. Eerdmans Publishing Co., 1957), pp. 32-47.

which the modernist has accepted. He breaks with the fundamentalist on the fact that he believes that the Biblical teaching, the Bible doctrine and ethics, must apply to the social scene, that there must be an application of this to society as much as there is an application of it to the individual man."[4]

A word of caution

Since such a wide range of divergence exists within neo-evangelicalism, it would be unwise to attempt to speak for them all. Some who are pleased to be so designated have more affinity to either neo-liberalism, neo-orthodoxy or fundamentalism than others. Some are to the right of center and others are to the extreme left of center. This treatment of the neo-evangelical doctrine of Scripture will seek to do justice to the divergent elements and give a fair appraisal of the common conceptions held by the majority. However, the weak views of Scripture here presented represent a significant and dangerous trend in the new evangelical camp. These views are not shared by all but they are shared by too many.

The Dissatisfactions in Bibliology

The church doctrine of Scripture

The church doctrine of Scripture has been often and ably presented. The historical development of the doctrines of revelation, inspiration and authority are squarely on the side of conservatism and need not be argued here. Through an accurate definition of the term *doctrine* as opposed to the term *dogma* and by reviewing the history of the doctrine it can be established that ". . . in the cases of revelation and inspiration a continuous, consistent, and practically unanimous doctrine essentially identical with the conservative doctrine of the present existed until almost 1800."[5]

The Bible doctrine of Scripture

It is always valuable to consider the beliefs of the church from its beginning. However, the Bible must be the final

---

[4] Ockenga, *op. cit.*, pp. 4-5.

[5] John A. Witmer, "A Critical Study of Current Trends in Bibliology" (unpublished Th. D. dissertation, Dallas Theological Seminary, 1953), p. 89.

court of appeal whether its teachings have been promoted in the church or not. That the Bible contains material for the formulation of a doctrine of Scripture has been presented above in the teachings of Christ. The Bible doctrine is also based upon the testimony of other portions of Scripture. The two classic passages presenting the Bible doctrine are 2 Timothy 3:16 and 2 Peter 1:20-21.[6]

Need for reexamination of Biblical inspiration

Some neo-evangelicals have questioned the dogmatic statements of those who hold to the doctrine of verbal plenary inspiration and thus the complete inerrancy of Scripture. The first public request for a reinvestigation of this view came in 1956 and was published in *Christian Life*.[7] Others have expressed a similar desire: ". . . our all important Protestant conviction of Biblical authority needs revitalizing."[8] The areas which Jewett lists as those needing revitalization are Scripture translation, Biblical authority and the doctrine of Scriptural inspiration. He desires this reinvestigation in accordance with helpful Biblical criticism.[9]

Carnell states his neo-evangelical position dogmatically: "Contemporary orthodoxy does very little to sustain the classical dialogue on inspiration. The fountain of new ideas has apparently run dry, for what was once a live issue in the church has now ossified into a theological tradition. As a result a heavy pall of fear hangs over the academic community. When a gifted professor tries to interact with the critical difficulties in the text, he is charged with disaffection, if not outright heresy. Orthodoxy forgets one important verdict of history: namely, that when truth is presented in a poor light, tomor-

---

[6] For an excellent discussion of these and others see Benjamin Breckinridge Warfield, *The Inspiration and Authority of the Bible* (Philadelphia: The Presbyterian and Reformed Publishing Co., 1948), pp. 131-68.

The recent attacks on these and other central texts by Beegle and Stevick have only further proven the subjective nature of the unbelieving opposition.

[7] "Is Evangelical Theology Changing?" *Christian Life*, XVII (March, 1956), 17.

[8] Paul King Jewett, "Biblical Authority a Crucial Issue in Protestantism," *United Evangelical Action*, VII (May 1, 1953), 9.

[9] *Ibid.*

row's leaders may embrace error on the single reason that it is more persuasively defended."[10]

The same writer expresses his own problem by attributing it to the whole of orthodoxy when he says, "The problem of inspiration is *still* a problem."[11]

The recent book by Ramm, *Special Revelation and the Word of God,* has much to commend it; yet the writer reveals a dissatisfaction with the fundamentalist doctrine of Scripture. Walvoord, in his review of the book, points this out: "Dr. Ramm feels that fundamentalism is guilty of incipient bibliolatry and that neo-orthodoxy is deficient in its concept of revelation as simply 'an encounter,' because revelation is 'both a knowing and an experience of the living God' (p. 7)."[12]

Ronald H. Nash has stated his dissatisfaction with the fundamentalist doctrine of Scripture and that of other neo-evangelicals very plainly: "Whether it be for good or ill, evangelicals are willing to reopen the subject of the inspiration of the Scriptures."[13]

Reasons for the dissatisfactions

From a careful study of neo-evangelical literature it appears that there are several reasons for the above interest in the reinvestigation of the doctrine of Scripture.

Probably the basic reason which has led to the reopening of the doctrine has been the neo-evangelical desire to present an intellectually acceptable position to those with whom the neo-evangelical desires to meet in theological table-talk. Walton, has stated this fact well: "This emphasis on scholarship appears to be basic to the New Evangelical movement. Concessions are made to science in the name of scholarly opinion. The doctrine of Biblical inspiration is reopened because of the influence of liberalism, especially neo-orthodoxy. Inspiration is further re-evaluated because of the problems that have been introduced by rationalistic textual criticism.

---

[10] Edward John Carnell, *The Case for Orthodox Theology* (Philadelphia: The Westminster Press, 1959), p. 110.

[11] *Ibid.*, p. 109.

[12] John F. Walvoord, Book Review of *Special Revelation and the Word of God* by Bernard Ramm, *Bibliotheca Sacra,* CXVIII (October, 1961), 347.

[13] Ronald H. Nash, *The New Evangelicalism* (Grand Rapids: Zondervan Publishing House, 1963), p. 35.

Ideas are exchanged with Liberal theologians because of an unwillingness to share the 'intellectual stagnation' that men like Carnell attribute to Fundamentalism."[14]

Ockenga has voiced this very desire on the part of neo-evangelicalism when he said that the neo-evangelical ". . . desires to win a new respectability for orthodoxy in the academic circles by producing scholars who can defend the faith on intellectual ground."[15]

Carnell's book, *The Case for Orthodox Theology*, is given over to a large extent to the downgrading of the fundamentalist intellectualism.[16]

These repentant fundamentalists express a dangerous subservience to science. The desire to gain intellectual acceptability has led to a friendly attitude toward science almost to the point of placing scholarship and science in the seat of authority. The threshold evolution of Edward John Carnell and the progressive creationism of Bernard Ramm are clear evidences of semantic delusions and needless concessions of the Word of God to science.

There are many evidences of this trend which reveals a reason for dissatisfaction but only a few need be cited here. Ockenga said in the Associated Press dispatch from Boston on December 8, 1957: "The evangelical believes that Christianity is intellectually defensible, that the Christian cannot be obscurantist in scientific questions pertaining to the creation, the age of man, the universality of the flood and other debatable Biblical questions. . . . The new evangelicalism is willing to face the intellectual problems and meet them in the framework of modern learning."[17]

Barnhouse expressed serious doubt of the validity of the historic orthodox interpretation of the first chapters of Genesis in his article "Adam and Modern Science." Speaking of the attitude which the Christian ought to take toward evolution, which Barnhouse called a model, he said: "The fact is

---

[14] Denis M. Walton, "An Identification of New Evangelicalism" (unpublished B. D. thesis, Central Conservative Baptist Theological Seminary, 1961), pp. 55-56.

[15] Harold John Ockenga, "Resurgent Evangelical Leadership," *Christianity Today*, V (October 10, 1960), 14.

[16] Carnell *op. cit.*, pp. 120ff.

[17] *Associated Press* (Boston), December 8, 1957, quoted in "The New Evangelicalism," *Christian Beacon*, XXII (January 9, 1958), 1.

(and there is no harm to confess it), that we Christians do not have a model that will synthetize the findings in nature and the statements of Scripture. And until we do, we have to be careful about pulling down the scientific model that is functioning so well in all the laboratories of the world. We do not have a better one. We live in hope that a better one will be forthcoming, but it has not yet been advanced."[18]

Bernard Ramm deals extensively with the relation of science and the inerrancy of Scripture and leaves the impression that Scripture ought to be interpreted in the light of science.[19] In another work the same writer voices an attitude which causes deep concern: "If the differences between the sciences and the Bible were to grow to a very large number and were of the most serious nature, it would be questionable if we could retain faith in Scripture. True, we may believe *some* of the Bible 'in spite of' science, but certainly the situation would change if we believed *all* of the Bible in spite of science."[20]

Carnell displayed his willingness to interpret the Bible in the light of science when he said: "The Genesis account implies an act of immediate creation, but the same account also implies that God made the world in six literal days; and since orthodoxy has given up the literal-day theory out of respect for geology, it would certainly forfeit no principle if it gave up the immediate-creation theory out of respect for paleontology. The two seem quite parallel."[21]

Certainly, Sanderson was right when he said, "Neo-Evangelicalism's 'friendly attitude toward science' has gone hand in hand with the 'reopening of the subject of Biblical inspiration.' "[22]

---

[18] Donald Grey Barnhouse, "Adam and Modern Science," *Eternity*, XI (May, 1960), 6.

[19] Bernard Ramm, *Protestant Biblical Interpretation* (Boston: W. A. Wilde Co., 1950), pp. 182-95.

[20] Bernard Ramm, *The Christian View of Science and Scripture* (Grand Rapids: Wm. B. Eerdmans Publishing Co., 1954), p. 29.

[21] Carnell, *op. cit.*, p. 95.

[22] John W. Sanderson, *Fundamentalism and Its Critics* (Philadelphia: The Sunday School Times Co., 1961), p. 12.

The Deviations in Bibliology

Some deviations have already been presented in the above discussion of the dissatisfactions which neo-evangelicals have with the doctrine of Scripture. There are other deviations which are clearly evident in the neo-evangelical approach.

Bibliology a secondary issue

This does not mean that the doctrine of Scripture does not receive consideration in neo-evangelicalism. It does mean though that, in relation to the soteriological and societal emphasis in neo-evangelicalism, Bibliology becomes a secondary issue. The importance of the Bible and yet its second place in relation to other considerations is disturbing. The neo-evangelical feels that one's views of the Bible should be in line with consistent modern discoveries. Ketcham accurately observed that the shifting of emphasis from Biblical authority to soteriology means that the neo-evangelical has shifted the emphases ". . . from the authority of Bible doctrine to the realm of human experience."[23]

Emphasis on creedal authority

Ockenga and Carnell both stress the necessity of connecting convictions with the classical creeds of the church. They do so to the extent that one gets the impression that creedal Christianity has always been Biblical Christianity which is not the case. Ockenga says, "First of all, the evangelical embraces creedal Christianity—Christianity as expressed in the confessions of the church . . . ."[24] Carnell claims that ". . . fundamentalists failed to connect their convictions with the classical creeds of the church."[25] He states elsewhere, "Orthodoxy is insecure because it neglects the majesty of its own traditions."[26] This type of attitude indicates a desire to place authority in the church and the creeds.

---

[23] Robert T. Ketcham, "A New Peril in Our Last Days," *Christian Beacon*, XXI (May 17, 1956), 6.

[24] Ockenga, *op. cit.*, p. 6.

[25] Carnell, *op. cit.*, p. 113.

[26] *Ibid.*, p. 127.

Emphasis on certain portions of the Bible

Another sign of weakness is the growing tendency to give the words of Christ and gospel passages a special place of priority over the rest of the Word of God. Carnell implies this in his criticism of Calvinism as cultic since it seldom appreciates the extent to which the New Testament ethic judges the truncated ethic of the Old Testament. This reveals clearly his desire to place more authority on some portions of the Bible than on others. The most obvious differentiation of the authority of Scripture comes when he practically discounts doctrine that is not clearly set forth in either Romans or Galations.[27]

Hesitancy to accept verbal inspiration

This fact has been noted by critics of the new evangelicalism for some time but was brought out clearly in a recent survey sponsored by *Christianity Today*. The survey revealed regarding theological beliefs among American clergymen that there were twelve per cent liberal, fourteen per cent neo-orthodox, thirty-five per cent fundamentalist and thirty-nine per cent conservative. The most alarming admission of the report was that the issue which distinguished the fundamentalist clergy from the conservative was the doctrine of Scripture. Fundamentalists subscribed to total or complete inerrancy whereas those who were considered conservatives either did not subscribe to total inerrancy or had doubts about the doctrine.[28]

DeWolf, a neo-liberal and thus one whom neo-evangelicals hope to win by their concessions, observed the revision of the doctrine of inspiration in neo-evangelical theology. He writes: "There is a noticeable, though indecisive change in the doctrine of Biblical inspiration and authority. Some of the new evangelicals, unlike most of the fundamentalists, avoid teaching 'verbal' inspiration of the Bible, stressing rather plenary or full inspiration. This marks a movement to a more flexible position."[29]

---

[27] *Ibid.*, pp. 58, 59, 66.

[28] "Theological Beliefs of American Clergymen," *Christianity Today*, VI (November 10, 1961), 11.

[29] L. Harold DeWolf, *Present Trends in Christian Thought* (New York: Association Press, 1960), p. 17.

Neo-evangelicalism cannot deny this because the word *verbal* is conspicuous by its absence in their discussions of inspiration. When writing of an inspired Bible neo-evangelicals often use the term *plenary inspiration* instead of verbal plenary inspiration.

Walvoord sees evidence of a conceptual theory of inspiration as opposed to a verbal plenary theory in Ramm's book, *Special Revelation and the Word of God.* He writes: "While clearly on the side of conservative orthodoxy, his treatment seems to embrace a dynamic or conceptual theory of inspiration as illustrated in the following sentence: 'Because the same thought (or meaning) can be expressed by different words the relationship is *dynamic* or *flexible* and not *fixed* or *mechanical*' (p. 178)."[30]

Agreeing with the neo-evangelical viewpoint Warren C. Young says: "Any type of verbal inspiration which fails to recognize the conceptual side will not carry much weight today."[31] Dewey M. Beegle who, according to Charles C. Ryrie, has given expression to the Biblical viewpoint of some neo-evangelicals,[32] not only expresses hesitancy to accept verbal inspiration but flatly denies it. "We need to remind ourselves that the verbal plenary formulation of inspiration is, after all, only a doctrine—a non-Biblical doctrine at that."[33]

These quotations should serve to illustrate the fact that neo-evangelicalism hesitates to accept verbal inspiration of the Scriptures. A notable and welcome exception to this has recently been expressed by Carl F. H. Henry. In a lively critique of *The Inspiration of Scripture* by Dewey M. Beegle, Henry states clearly his acceptance of the verbal inerrancy of Scripture. He states: "The Scriptures assert that inspiration extended not only to chosen persons but to their sacred writings, and that the very words derive their unique authority from this supernatural superintendence."[34]

---

[30] Walvoord, *loc. cit.*

[31] Alva J. McClain, "Is Theology Changing in the Conservative Camp?" *The Brethren Missionary Herald,* XIX (February 23, 1957), 19.

[32] Charles C. Ryrie, Book Review of *The New Evangelicalism* by Ronald H. Nash, *Bibliotheca Sacra,* CXXI (January-March, 1964), 68.

[33] Dewey M. Beegle, *The Inspiration of Scripture* (Philadelphia: The Westminster Press, 1963), p. 187.

[34] Carl F. H. Henry (ed.), "Yea, Hath God Said . . .?" *Christianity Today,* VII (April 26, 1963), 47.

Tendency to distinguish between inspiration and inerrancy

While Henry's public admission of verbal inspiration and inerrancy is to be welcomed one reads with mixed emotions the words of hesitancy which come from the pen of Everett F. Harrison: "Unquestionably the Bible teaches its own inspiration. It is the Book of God. *It does not require us to hold inerrancy,* [italics not in original] though this is a natural corollary of full inspiration. The phenomena which present difficulties are not to be dismissed or underrated. They have driven many sincere believers in the truthworthiness of the Bible as a spiritual guide to hold a modified position on the non-revelation material. Every man must be persuaded in his own mind."[35]

Here is expressed hesitancy to accept total inerrancy in all the Bible—revelational and non-revelational. Also, Harrison places the responsibility of determining the Bible's view of its own inerrancy at the mercy of man's mind.

Edward John Carnell confessed his own problem in relation to proposed theological and historical errors in Scripture in his conversation with Karl Barth in Chicago. Carnell's question to Barth was, " 'How does Dr. Barth harmonize his appeal to Scripture as the objective Word of God with his admission that Scripture is sullied by errors, theological as well as historical or factual?' Carnell confessed parenthetically that 'this is a problem for me, too.' "[36]

An attempt to modify Carnell's position and poor testimony before Barth appeared in *Christianity Today,* June 8, 1962. The article implied that Dr. Clark of Butler University, who had written the first article, was left with the impression that Carnell did not believe in an inerrant Scripture. Incidentally, Clark is not alone in that impression. In the same article, Carnell's statement of his view of Scripture to the Fuller Seminary chapel was given. After admitting his problems Carnell said: ". . . I now believe and always have believed plenary inspiration of Scripture and the inerrancy of Scripture."[37] This statement does not free Carnell from the

[35] Everett F. Harrison, "The Phenomena of Scripture," *Revelation and the Bible,* ed. Carl F. H. Henry (Grand Rapids: Baker Book House, 1958), p. 250.

[36] "Special Report: Encountering Barth in Chicago," *Christianity Today,* VI (May 11, 1962), 36.

[37] "Carnell on Scripture," *Christianity Today,* VI (June 8, 1962), 20.

charge of failing to believe in verbal inspiration and total inerrancy of Scripture, even non-revealed matters, because it is lacking in two great essentials. It is lacking by the omission of the word *verbal* and the word *complete* inerrancy of Scripture.

The tendency to distinguish between inspiration and inerrancy is very obvious in Nash's recent work. He evidently prefers the term "adequacy" to "inerrancy." He conveniently evades the issue of inerrancy by cluttering it with matters of translation difficulties. "The autographs may have been inerrant while later translations and versions are adequate, albeit not perfect, representations of the original message."[38] He further states, "Contemporary evangelicals are pointing out that inspiration and inerrancy are not equivalent concepts."[39] And again, "Strictly speaking, the Bible does not teach the inerrancy of its original manuscripts."[40]

With special reference to the words of Harrison cited above but with general reference to all who express this distinction between inspiration and inerrancy, Ryrie states: "In other words, some, because of apparent difficulties in the Bible (such as historical and chronological problems) are concluding that these sections are not inerrant though inspired. One hears more and more these days: 'I believe the Bible is inspired, but I cannot believe that it is without error.' Inspiration, yes; verbal inspiration, no. Why is it so? One cannot see motives, but for some it is the result of honest wrestling with problems which have shaken their faith. For others, one cannot help but feel that it is part of the current worship of intellectualism as a sacred cow and a necessary step in achieving the approbation of godless intellectuals so-called."[41]

J. Barton Payne expressed the same objection to an attempt on the part of Carnell in his *Case* book to profess to believe Scripture and at the same time to question its concrete data. In fact, Payne titled his article in critique of Carnell's

---

[38] *Ibid.*, p. 66.
[39] *Ibid.*, p. 75.
[40] *Ibid.*, p. 76.
[41] Charles C. Ryrie, "The Importance of Inerrancy," *Bibliotheca Sacra*, CXX (April-June, 1963), 140.

view of Scripture "Hermeneutics as a Cloak for the Denial of Scripture."[42]

This tendency to distinguish between inspiration and complete inerrancy has been called the "double-revelation theory" by John C. Whitcomb.[43] In his criticism of the theory he explains it is as follows: "Briefly stated, this theory maintains that God has given to man two revelations of truth, each of which is fully authoritative in its own realm: the revelation of God in Scripture and the revelation of God in nature. . . . The theologian is the God-appointed interpreter of Scripture and the scientist is the God-appointed interpreter of nature, and each has specialized tools for determining the true meaning of the particular book of revelation which he is called upon to study."[44]

This type of approach to Scripture which is being advocated by neo-evangelical scholars[45] allows them to apply inspiration and inerrancy only to matters of faith and life in the scriptures and not to peripheral matters. Peripheral matters would include whatever the individual decides is not a matter of faith and life such as problems of the origin of the universe, the solar system, the earth, man, the magnitude and effects of the flood, minor historical details, grammatical constructions, etc.

Beegle's extreme viewpoint regarding Scripture is the end product of the neo-evangelical desire to accommodate the Bible to science. He writes: "The inductive evidence of the New Testament indicates that Jesus taught a strong doctrine of inspiration and authority of Scripture, yet without claiming inerrancy."[46] Again he says: "But minor historical

---

[42] J. Barton Payne, "Hermeneutics as a Cloak for the Denial of Scripture," *Bulletin of the Evangelical Theological Society* (Fall, 1960), p. 99.

[43] John C. Whitcomb, *The Origin of the Solar System*: Biblical Inerrancy and the Double Revelation Theory, (Presbyterian and Reformed Publishing Co., 1964.)

[44] *Ibid.*, p. 4.

[45] See the following: Carnell, *op. cit.*, p. 111; Harrison, *op. cit.*, p. 249; H. N. Ridderbos, *When the Time Had Fully Come* (Grand Rapids: Wm. B. Eerdmans Publishing Co., 1957), p. 90; Ramm, *op. cit.*, p. 104; Russell L. Mixter, *Evolution and Christian Thought Today* (Grand Rapids: Wm. B. Eerdmans Publishing Co., 1959), pp. 34-35, 48.

[46] Beegle, *op. cit.*, p. 170.

errors in Scripture invalidate neither our faith nor true doctrine."[47]

Joseph A. Hill, in a report of Dr. George Stob's view of infallibility presented as a lecture at Trinity College in Worth, Illinois, clearly distinguished the neo-evangelical view of inspiration and the traditional orthodox position set forth by Warfield and more recently by Edward J. Young in *Thy Word Is Truth.* Hill writes: "There are in the present controversy two theories as to the nature of inspiration. These are as follows: 1. Inspiration makes certain that we have an authoritative record of all that God wanted to make known. But it was not God's intention or purpose to secure inerrancy in peripheral matters. 'Peripheral matters' include Scriptural data which have nothing to do with faith and life, such as minor historical details, grammatical constructions, and the like. 2. The other view is that inspiration applies to all the data of Scripture, including peripheral matters. Every word of the Bible, all grammatical points and every historical detail, however trivial, are God-breathed. According to this view the Bible is free from all error, discrepancy, and inaccuracy."[48]

There have been some notable and welcome exceptions to the weak view of Scripture among neo-evangelicals. In fact, a rift seems to be developing within the new evangelical school of thought over this very issue of the inerrancy of Scripture. Two excellent expressions of dissatisfaction with any attempt to believe in the inspiration of Scripture and not the total inerrancy of Scripture have appeared recently in the *Bulletin of the Evangelical Theological Society.*[49]

While those evangelicals who have adopted a weak view of Scripture may find refuge in the views of others, they cannot find support for their views in the teaching of Christ or the Bible. One's view of Scripture must not be derived or defended merely from the views of others, however high a regard for Scripture they may or may not have. The

---

[47] *Ibid.*

[48] Joseph A. Hill, "Dr. George Stob on Infallibility," *Torch and Trumpet,* IX (January, 1960), 6.

[49] Harold Lindsell, "An Historian Looks at Inerrancy," *Bulletin of the Evangelical Theological Society* (Winter, 1965) and John Warwick Montgomery, "Inspiration and Inerrancy: a New Departure," *Bulletin of the Evangelical Theological Society* (Spring, 1965).

conservative must find his view of Scripture from the Scriptures.

The subjectivity in the mediating voices among the new evangelicals may not be as decided as in the neo-orthodox and neo-liberal views but it is there nonetheless. And so is the very real danger, therefore, of departure from other orthodox tenets of the faith. History bears solemn testimony to the fact that the rejection of Biblical doctrines has always begun with a rejection of the total and absolute authority of the Bible.

Harold Lindsell admits the presence of some among the new evangelicals who no longer believe in an inerrant Scripture. "Today there are those who have been numbered among the New Evangelicals, some of whom possess the keenest minds and have acquired the apparati of scholarship, who have broken, or are in the process of breaking, with the doctrine of an inerrant Scripture."[50] The same writer dons the role of a prophet as he predicts a dangerous future for those who hold such a weak view of Scripture and consequently for the church as well. One must fearfully agree with his prediction. "One can predict with almost fatalistic certainty that in due course of time the moderating evangelicals who deny inerrancy will adopt new positions such as belief in the multiple authorship of Isaiah, the late date of Daniel, the idea that the first eleven chapters of Genesis are myth and saga; and then these critical conclusions will spill over into the New Testament and when the same principles of higher criticisms are applied, this can only lead to a scrapping of the facticity of the resurrection, etc. This has ever been the historical movement and there is nothing to suppose that such a repetitive process will not follow."[51]

Deviations from Christ's view

Whatever the motives may be and however high a view of Scripture these neo-evangelicals may claim to espouse, the deviations cited above represent serious differences with the view of Scripture presented by Christ. These differences are dangerous. They not only are inconsistent with the high view of Scripture of itself and the high view of Scripture presented

---

[50] Lindsell, *ibid.*, p. 10.

[51] *Ibid.*, p. 11.

by Christ but if carried to their logical conclusions may well evaporate the need for any special revelation from God. If God may not be trusted in the things He has revealed which do not relate to faith and life how may He be trusted at all? How is one to decide what is a matter of faith and life and what is not?

The Lord's teaching regarding the abiding character of the very words of Scripture including the letters and parts of letters making up the words (Matt. 5:17-19) presents His teaching of complete verbal inerrancy if it presents anything at all. Also, Christ's emphasis upon the impossibility of annulling or breaking the words of Scripture is absolutely meaningless if He did not teach verbal plenary inspiration and thus complete inerrancy both in that which was revealed directly by God and that which might be classified as non-revelational material (John 10:33-36). The Lord went so far as to teach the inerrancy not only of words but also He extended it to the grammatical form of the verb (Matt. 22:32).

Christ made no distinction between facts of history, geography, science or theology. He referred to them all—to that which was directly revealed by God and to that which was not so revealed—and always endorsed the Scriptures with the divine authority which they possessed and invested them with His own divine authority (Matt. 5:17, 18; Luke 24:44; John 10:34, 35).

Thus Christ is not completely nor accurately preached unless His view of Scripture be accepted in spite of problems which the human mind may encounter. There were problems of translation and distance from the originals when Christ spoke; yet this did not keep Him from accepting the Scriptures in their entirety as the verbally inerrant Word of God.

The Battle For the Bible Continues

Since the first edition of this book in 1966 the battle over the Bible among professed evangelicals has enlarged considerably. Two recent books reveal clearly the warfare over the Word of God among would-be evangelicals. The first of these, *The Battle For the Bible*, was written by Harold Lindsell while he was editor of *Christianity Today*. The second, a response to Lindsell's book, is entitled *Biblical Authority* and was edited by Jack Rogers of Fuller Theological Seminary.

As these books reveal, two different views of the extent of the Bible's inspiration are held by those who claim to be evangelical. The fact is, this dual view has been true for some time, as noted earlier in this chapter.

In response to the inerrancy debate among those who profess to believe the Bible, a new organization was formed in September, 1977. The International Council of Biblical Inerrancy came into being as a result of a meeting of thirty prominent evangelical leaders and scholars. It is a ten-year effort to study and defend the doctrine of Biblical inerrancy. The council is to stress the importance of the doctrine of total inerrancy and to demonstrate that those who deny it are not true to the Bible's witness to itself or to the historic evangelical mainstream.

Already in 1956 neo-evangelicals were calling for a "reopening of the subject of Biblical inspiration."[52] At that time this intention was viewed as "just a pebble in the pond of conservative theology" which "could expand to the bombshell of mid-century evangelicalism."[53] And as we now know, that is precisely what has taken place.

In his foreword to *The Battle For the Bible,* Harold J. Ockenga acknowledged these two prominent views regarding the Bible:

> The first view considers all of Scripture to be inspired and true, including the historical, geographical, and scientific teaching. The second view holds that only the Bible teaching on salvation-history and doctrine is true. The Bible is authoritative for faith and practice only. Some who adopt the second view would say that the Bible is plenarily inspired, but that God intended the writers to use their limited knowledge—which is erroneous—in making nonrevelatory statements.[54]

It is not a secret that the evangelical world is being fragmented and divided more and more over the Bible, its self-

---

[52] "Is Evangelical Theology Changing?" *Christian Life,* XVII (Mar. 1956), 17.

[53] Ibid.

[54] Harold Lindsell, *The Battle For the Bible* (Grand Rapids: Zondervan Pub. House, 1976), p. i.

claimed source of authority. In his controversial book, Lindsell confirms this:

> Fundamentalists and evangelicals (both of whom have been traditionally committed to an infallible or inerrant Scripture) have long been noted for their propagation and defense of an infallible Bible. But more recently, among those who call themselves evangelicals, there has been a marked departure from the viewpoint held by them for so long. More and more organizations and individuals historically committed to an infallible Scripture have been embracing and propagating the view that the Bible has errors in it. This movement away from the historic standpoint has been most noticeable among those often labeled neo-evangelicals. This change of position with respect to the infallibility of the Bible is widespread and has occurred in evangelical denominations, Christian colleges, theological seminaries, publishing houses, and learned societies.[55]

What is meant by a totally inerrant Bible?

Those who believe all of Scripture to be God-breathed and therefore true, believe the Bible is totally inerrant, or without error. This applies to all the Bible states including its historical, geographical, and scientific teaching.

The opposing view of those who claim to be evangelical (referred to above by Ockenga) is a very different view of the Bible. It is the view which says that only what the Bible teaches about salvation and things related directly to the Christian life is without error or inerrant. All the other matters recorded in the Bible, which are viewed as peripheral matters, are not necessarily without error.

In his critique of the totally inerrant view of the Bible. Clark Pinnock revealed the opposing view held by evangelicals:

> Instead of placing emphasis upon the saving truth of the Bible to bear witness to Christ, attention is focused rather on the precise accuracy of minor details. This unfortunate development does not do justice to the kind of book the Bible is. Minute inerrancy may be a central issue for the telephone book but not for psalms,

[55] Ibid., p. 20.

> proverbs, apocalyptic, and parables. Inerrancy just does not focus attention correctly where the Bible is concerned.[56]

It may be well to state both the positive and negative aspects of what we mean when we say we believe in the total inerrancy of Scripture.

On the positive side the total inerrancy of the Bible means it does not lie, it does not make mistakes in any of its affirmations. Scripture possesses the quality of absolute freedom from error in all its pronouncements. None of the Bible's statements are contrary to fact. The human writers of Scripture recorded accurately precisely what the Holy Spirit desired them to write—no more and no less.

Does this view of Scripture demand word for word agreement in parallel passages? No, it only means each account must tell the truth. Does this view mean that every word of the Bible was dictated by God to the writers? No, there is too much evidence of differences in style among the writers. And yet it is true that considerable portions of the Bible were dictated directly by God. Are there not errors recorded in the Bible? Indeed there are. Mistakes are recorded while the record is without mistakes. To what does this total inerrancy apply? Does it extend to translations and versions? No, it applies only to the original autographs of Scripture. They were the product of the creative breath of God.

True, we do not have those originals and therefore they cannot be used to prove they are either inerrant or errant. What we do have however in the many copies of those originals is the Word of God insofar as it approximates the autographs. And of course if the original autographs were not altogether inerrant what hope have we that in our English Bible we have the Word of God? What about the many copies of those originals upon which our English Bibles are based?

> Are these copies, however, hopelessly corrupt? For our part, we are convinced that they are not. We believe that the Bible which we have is accurate and that it

---

[56] Clark Pinnock, "Three Views of the Bible in Contemporary Theology," *Biblical Authority* edited by Jack Rogers. (Waco: Word Books, 1977), p. 67.

> is a remarkably close approximation to the original manuscripts.
>
> Suppose that a schoolteacher writes a letter to the President of the United States. To her great joy she receives a personal reply. It is a treasure which she must share with her pupils and so she dictates the letter to them. They are in the early days of their schooling, and spelling is not yet one of their strong points. In his copy of the letter Johnny has misspelled a few words. Mary has forgotten to cross her t's and to dot her i's. Billy has written one or two words twice, and Peter has omitted a word now and then. Nevertheless, despite all these flaws about thirty copies of the President's letter have been made. Unfortunately, the teacher misplaces the original and cannot find it. To her great sorrow it is gone. She does not have the copy which came directly from the President's pen; she must be content with those that the children have made.
>
> Will anyone deny that she has the words of the President? Does she not have his message, in just those words in which he wrote it to her? True enough, there are some minor mistakes in the letters, but the teacher may engage in the science of textual criticism and correct them. She may correct the misspelled words, and she may write in those words which have been omitted and cross out those which are superfluous. Without any serious difficulty she may indeed restore the original.[57]

Does a belief in the total inerrancy of the Bible mean there are no difficulties in the Bible? No, indeed it does not. We must distinguish between a difficulty and a contradiction, however. There are difficulties and seeming contradictions. But since the Bible claims to be from God who cannot lie we believe Him and seek to solve those difficulties. Because we cannot solve every problem in the Bible does not mean there is no solution to those problems. More and more of the problems in Scripture are being solved all the time. There are no new problems which contemporary critics have discovered. And what is more, valid solutions were offered long ago for

---

[57] Edward J. Young, *Thy Word Is Truth* (Grand Rapids: Wm. B. Eerdmans Publishing Co., 1967), p. 57.

the existing problems.[58] When we come upon a problem or apparent contradiction in the Bible to which we do not have a satisfactory solution we wait in faith, believing what God has told us about His Word.

The belief in a totally inerrant Bible is based upon the Bible's own claims for itself, and the claims of the Saviour, and not upon the alleged contradictions in it. Those who do not believe in the total inerrancy of Scripture do not begin with its claims but rather with the phenomena of Scripture.

Why is a totally inerrant Bible rejected today?

Unfortunately, the belief that the Bible is not totally inerrant is found even among evangelicals. Liberals, of course, have always believed it. From the beginning they rejected the Bible's inerrancy because they rejected its inspiration. They were consistent in that. After all, if something is not God-breathed it surely will not be without error.

Disbelief in the inerrancy of Scripture is rather new among evangelicals. The question is, Why have evangelicals begun to doubt Scriptural inerrancy? Have there been some new discoveries to discredit the Bible? No. Are there some new problems for which there are no satisfactory solutions? No.

Evangelicals who reject the total inerrancy of the Bible do so because they feel the view does not take seriously enough the human side of Scripture.

> The prime theological issue which became evident in our survey of options on biblical authority is the need to maintain with equal force both the humanity and the divinity of the word of Scripture.[59]

Over and over again we hear this from those who reject total inerrancy: since the writers of Scripture were human, error is possible in those things they wrote which were not directly revealed to them by God. In response it must be said that the same sinful humanity touched all of Scripture. On

---

58 See John W. Haley, *An Examination of the Alleged Discrepancies of the Bible*. (Nashville: Gospel Advocate Company, 1967).

59 Pinnock, p. 71.

what basis therefore may I be sure that *anything* they wrote is free from error? The usual answer is: When the human penmen of Scripture wrote what was directly revealed to them about the central theme and purpose of Scripture they wrote inerrantly. And what, we ask, is the central theme and purpose of Scripture? Salvation and the Christian life comes the answer. And who decides when matters in Scripture are central and when they are peripheral? And the embarrassing answer must be, the interpreter of Scripture. From those who embrace a totally inerrant Bible the response comes loud and clear—that method is far too subjective and we prefer to let the Bible speak for itself.

> If Scripture itself professes to be inerrant only with respect to revelational or salvatory truth, where is the evidence for this to be found? Not in Scripture. For when the Word of God speaks of its trustworthiness, at no point does it include any limitation. Nor does it indicate that some parts of Scripture are thus to be trusted and other parts are not. If there is any doctrine of infallibility based upon the biblical data, it must include all of Scripture or none of it.[60]

I am convinced that there is one basic reason underlying all other reasons for the rejection of the inerrancy of the Bible among self-confessed evangelicals. That reason is related to the attempt to accommodate the Bible to science, falsely so-called, and modern unbelieving scholarship. The rejection is an evidence of the tendency to succumb to the worship of intellectualism and thereby to fail to take God at His Word. This does not mean those who hold such a view of Scripture are not sincere. Many of them have no doubt embraced their view in answer to honest inquiry. But the fact remains that underlying the initial rejection there was the attempt to embrace a less objectionable view of the Bible, one that would be more harmonious with the naturalist world view.

Why is it so important to hold to a totally inerrant Bible?

God cannot lie. To reject what He has said about His Word is to accuse Him of falsehood. How can an errant Bible

[60] Lindsell, p. 32.

be God's revelation? How can it be God-breathed? How can it possibly be authoritative and therefore trustworthy? No, God does not lead man astray. To reject a totally inerrant Scripture is to cast aspersions on the very character of God. God's Word and His character are at stake in this debate.

How can Scripture possibly be inerrant in some parts and errant in others at the same time? In a book which claims God as its author, inspiration must extend to all its parts. If it does not, how does one go about determining what is and what is not God-breathed and therefore free from error? If some of it is inerrant why is not all of it inerrant, since both the revelational and the non-revelational matters were touched by the same human frailty. An errant inspired Bible is a meaningless designation. An errant Bible which claims to be God's Word is Biblically, theologically, and philosophically indefensible.

In a general way every Scriptural claim for inspiration is also a claim for inerrancy. It would be well at this point for the reader to review pages 60 to 77 in this book where Christ's teaching of the inspiration of Scripture is presented. There can be no mistaking it—the Saviour believed in a totally inerrant Bible. He made no distinction between central and peripheral issues, between scientific and salvation matters. For Him all the Scriptures existing in His day constituted the inerrant Word of God.

Bible believers do not worship the Bible. But they do worship the God of the Bible. They believe that what He said about the Bible is just as true as what He said about His Son. He can be trusted! Lovers of the Book also cling to what God's Son, the Saviour, said about the Bible. They believe Him, too. In fact these people think it highly inconsistent and well nigh inexplicable that anyone should say he accepts the Saviour for all He claimed to be but not what He said about the Scriptures.

Believers in a totally inerrant written Word of God are fully cognizant of the fact that the ones whom the Spirit chose to write that Word were fully human. Not for a moment do they think the human penmen were sinless either. But along with this belief they also affirm that the same Spirit who chose men to write supernaturally kept them from all error and omission in all that they wrote.

Was not Christ, the Living Word of God, also touched by sinful humanity? Are we to believe then that because Mary was a member of Adam's sinful race the Saviour was therefore errant? If the involvement of sinful humanity in the production of the written Word of God means it must be errant in certain places why does not the same principle apply also to the Living Word of God? If the presence of humanity in relation to the Scriptures makes inerrancy impossible it would seem that the same would be true of the Saviour, making Him less than sinless.

Chapter VIII

CONCLUSION

The purpose of this work was to set forth the Saviour's teaching concerning the Scriptures and to compare that teaching with selected contemporary views.

It has been established that Christ's use of the Scriptures was constant and extensive. He relied solely upon the canonical Scriptures and expressed serious objections to the traditions of men which contradicted the Scriptures. His usage illustrates His profound respect for the inherent authority and irrevocable finality of Scripture. He used the Scriptures for His own needs and the needs of those to whom He ministered. His usage extended to the whole Old Testament in recognition of the threefold division of the Hebrew canon. The methods of interpretation and application employed by Christ were seen to be in complete harmony with the historical, grammatical, literal method of interpretation and application. The high and exalted view of Scripture espoused and proclaimed by Christ was the same when He was alone or in the presence of many. It was the same at the beginning of His ministry as it was at the end. It was the same after the resurrection as it was before.

According to the teaching of Christ Scripture originated with God. He taught clearly that the Word of God was the product of God's revelation. For Him what the Old Testament declared in the words of its human writers God said. Christ taught that God not only revealed Himself in acts of history but also that He spoke; He made Himself known in words. It has been established that Christ's emphasis upon what was written establishes the fact that He believed the revelation extended to the very words of Scripture. In this same connection it has been set forth that Christ recognized His place in the Scriptures and taught that Moses and all the prophets wrote and spoke of Him.

Since Christ taught that Scripture was of divine origination it is not difficult to see how He taught the inspiration of Scripture. Through the citation of specific passages the fact has been established that Christ accepted and clearly taught the verbal plenary inspiration of Scripture. This fact obviously led to His teaching of the complete inerrancy of Scripture. The inerrancy of Scripture deduced from His teaching extended not only to matters of faith and life but to what today would hardly be considered a matter of faith and life—the jot and tittle of Scripture. Thus Scripture not only teaches its own inspiration but also its own inerrancy—and that from the life of the Saviour. He not only taught the complete inspiration of the entire Old Testament but also made provision in His teaching for the inspiration of the New Testament. His promise of the guiding and controlling power of the Holy Spirit guaranteed the same divine inspiration to the New Testament as He attributed to the Old.

While almost every reference of Christ to the Old Testament Scriptures reveals His teaching of its authority, special emphasis was given to His specific teaching of the authority of Scripture. Considerable emphasis was placed upon the authority of Christ because of the current trend to discount the authority of Scripture and replace it with His own authority. The untenable nature of such a position was revealed since Christ subjected Himself and His divine authority to the authority of the Scriptures. Special attention was devoted to the teaching of Christ recorded in John 10:33-36 where He placed His divine stamp of approval upon the very words of the Old Testament and attributed to them irrevocable authority.

Three of the major chapters of this work were devoted to contemporary views of Scripture as they compared with Christ's view. It has been established that neo-orthodoxy falls far short of accepting the view of Scripture endorsed by the Christ it claims to exalt. Neo-liberalism, it has been shown, also differs drastically in its doctrine of Scripture with the teaching of Christ. In the areas of revelation, inspiration, and authority these contemporary views are in direct opposition to the view of Christ. They deny what He proclaimed. Their subjective nature and refusal to accept the Bible's witness to its own inspiration and authority is clearly evident. They have substituted their own rationalistic subjectivity for the authority of Christ and the Scriptures.

While the view of Scripture held by segments of conservative theology known as neo-evangelicalism is not to be equated with the views discussed above, a serious deviation from Christ's view and a trend toward subjectivism within the movement has been noted. Neo-evangelical subjectivity has been exposed in its emphasis upon certain portions of Scripture as though they were more inspired than others, in its hesitancy to accept verbal inspiration, in its failure to acknowledge the Bible's teaching of its own inerrancy and in its tendency to relegate parts of Scripture to matters of faith and life as inerrant and other parts as not necessarily inerrant. The non-revelational theory of inspiration endorsed by increasing numbers of neo-evangelicals has been dealt with and its serious disagreements with Christ's view revealed. The subjective element in such a view of Scripture is not as broad and encompassing as it is in neo-orthodoxy and neo-liberalism but it is subjectivism nonetheless.

We have seen that Christ's view of Scripture is the same view which the apostles and early church accepted and proclaimed. It has been demonstrated that no one can rightly claim Christ who does not adopt His view of Scripture. If what He said about the Scriptures was not authoritative how is one to decide when and to what extent anything He said is authoritative? "The evidence is clear: To Christ the Old Testament was true, authoritative, inspired. To Him the God of the Old Testament was the living God and the teaching of the Old Testament was the teaching of the living God. To Him, what Scripture said, God said."[1]

---

[1] J. W. Wenham, *Our Lord's View of the Old Testament* (London: The Tyndale Press, 1953), p. 32.

INDEX OF SCRIPTURE

I. Old Testament

II. New Testament

GENERAL INDEX